CAMBRIDGE LIBRARY COLLECTION

Books of enduring scholarly value

British and Irish History, Seventeenth and Eighteenth Centuries

The books in this series focus on the British Isles in the early modern period, as interpreted by eighteenth- and nineteenth-century historians, and show the shift to 'scientific' historiography. Several of them are devoted exclusively to the history of Ireland, while others cover topics including economic history, foreign and colonial policy, agriculture and the industrial revolution. There are also works in political thought and social theory, which address subjects such as human rights, the role of women, and criminal justice.

The Rural Economy of the West of England

Between 1787 and 1798, the agricultural writer and land agent William Marshall (1745–1818) published a number of works on the rural economies of England, covering Norfolk, his native Yorkshire, Gloucestershire, the Midlands and the South. This two-volume study appeared in 1796 and investigated the farming, geography, public works and produce of districts in Devon, Somerset, Dorset and Cornwall. Volume 2 looks in detail at the upland areas of Cornwall and Devon, at Dartmoor, North Devon, the vales of Exeter and Taunton, and West Dorset. The coverage includes aspects of the laws surrounding land ownership, the chemistry of the soil, notes on the dairy industry, and suggested improvements to farming practices. The result is a richly detailed survey of the area in the Georgian period and an important record of rural and agricultural life, so often overlooked by other contemporary chroniclers.

Cambridge University Press has long been a pioneer in the reissuing of out-of-print titles from its own backlist, producing digital reprints of books that are still sought after by scholars and students but could not be reprinted economically using traditional technology. The Cambridge Library Collection extends this activity to a wider range of books which are still of importance to researchers and professionals, either for the source material they contain, or as landmarks in the history of their academic discipline.

Drawing from the world-renowned collections in the Cambridge University Library and other partner libraries, and guided by the advice of experts in each subject area, Cambridge University Press is using state-of-the-art scanning machines in its own Printing House to capture the content of each book selected for inclusion. The files are processed to give a consistently clear, crisp image, and the books finished to the high quality standard for which the Press is recognised around the world. The latest print-on-demand technology ensures that the books will remain available indefinitely, and that orders for single or multiple copies can quickly be supplied.

The Cambridge Library Collection brings back to life books of enduring scholarly value (including out-of-copyright works originally issued by other publishers) across a wide range of disciplines in the humanities and social sciences and in science and technology.

The Rural Economy
of the West of England

*Including Devonshire, and Parts of Somersetshire,
Dorsetshire, and Cornwall*

VOLUME 2

WILLIAM MARSHALL

CAMBRIDGE
UNIVERSITY PRESS

CAMBRIDGE
UNIVERSITY PRESS

University Printing House, Cambridge, CB2 8BS, United Kingdom

Published in the United States of America by Cambridge University Press, New York

Cambridge University Press is part of the University of Cambridge.
It furthers the University's mission by disseminating knowledge in the pursuit of
education, learning and research at the highest international levels of excellence.

www.cambridge.org
Information on this title: www.cambridge.org/9781108067546

© in this compilation Cambridge University Press 2014

This edition first published 1796
This digitally printed version 2014

ISBN 978-1-108-06754-6 Paperback

This book reproduces the text of the original edition. The content and language reflect
the beliefs, practices and terminology of their time, and have not been updated.

Cambridge University Press wishes to make clear that the book, unless originally published
by Cambridge, is not being republished by, in association or collaboration with, or
with the endorsement or approval of, the original publisher or its successors in title.

THE

RURAL ECONOMY

OF THE

WEST OF ENGLAND:

INCLUDING

DEVONSHIRE;

AND PARTS OF

SOMERSETSHIRE,

DORSETSHIRE,

AND

CORNWALL.

TOGETHER WITH

MINUTES IN PRACTICE.

By Mr. MARSHALL.

VOL. II.

LONDON:

Printed for G. NICOL, Bookfeller to His Majefty; Pall Mall;
G. G. and J. ROBINSON, Paternofter Row;
and J. DEBRETT, Piccadilly.

M,DCC,XCVI.

CONTENTS

OF THE

SECOND VOLUME.

―――――――

DISTRICT THE THIRD.

THE

MOUNTAINS

OF

GORNWALL AND DEVONSHIRE.

PREFATORY REMARKS, I.

―――――――

EXCURSION IN CORNWALL.

     Subsoil,

BODMIN to BUCKLAND, 10.

CONTENTS.

a 3   DARTMORE,

D A R T M O R E,

AND ITS

UNCULTIVATED ENVIRONS.

IMPROVE-a 4   DISTRICT

DISTRICT THE FOURTH.

NORTH DEVONSHIRE.

DISTRICT THE FIFTH.

THE

VALE OF EXETER.

The

The RURAL ECONOMY of this Diſtrict.

———————

DISTRICT THE SIXTH.

THE DAIRY DISTRICT

O F

WEST DORSETSHIRE.

The AGRICULTURE of this Diftrict.

DISTRICT

DISTRICT THE SEVENTH,

THE

VALE OF TAUNTON,

&c. &c.

BLACK-

RETROSPECTIVE VIEW

OF THE

WEST OF ENGLAND.

Training

MINUTES

I N

WEST DEVONSHIRE.

MIN.

Min.

MIN.

CONTENTS.   xxiii

On

DISTRICT

DISTRICT THE THIRD.

THE

MOUNTAINS

OF

CORNWALL AND DEVONSHIRE.

PREFATORY REMARKS.

THE MATERIALS which I collected, respecting these Mountain Tracts, were obtained in different ways.

What relates to CORNWALL, I gathered in an EXCURSION; undertaken for the purpose of gaining some general ideas respecting this remote part of the Island.

But, with respect to DARTMORE, and its uncultivated Environs, the information I am possessed of arose INCIDENTALLY; without any premeditated plan of survey.

VOL. II.   B   Indeed,

Indeed, thefe wild uncultivated lands refemble, fo much, the mountainous parts of
Scotland, and the North of England, on
which the broad lines of nature remain
unobliterated, that a minute examination
was the lefs required, by one who has been
accuftomed to read her works; and whofe
only defire, in this inftance, was to extract
a few leading facts.

My fources of information being thus
diftinct, I will preferve the materials feparate, and, firft offer a Tranfcript of my
CORNISH JOURNAL, as it was haftily
formed, at the time of making the Excurfion (in AUGUST 1791); whether it
relate to the MOUNTAINS or the Low-
LANDS of Cornwall.

AN

AN

EXCURSION

IN

CORNWALL.

THIS Excurfion was made,---by CAL-
LINGTON and LESKARD, to BODMIN;
and back by LAUNCESTON and TAVIS-
TOCK.

BUCKLAND TO BODMIN.

The ELEVATION of the Country, in this
ride, is high: the road leads, moft of the
way, between the Mountains, and the
broken cultivated Country toward the Sea;
and, in paffing between Lefkard and Bodmin, it croffes over the chain of Mountains
which run through this Peninfula; but not
in an elevated part. Some very high hills
are feen to the North of the road:---
"Hinkftone," a depreffed Cone, with a

Profpect

Profpect Houfe on the top, is feen at great diftances; but a hill weftward of it, over-looking Callington, is faid to be the higheft land, in the County. Many ragged *Tors*, of the true mountain caft, are feen in this ride.

CLIMATURE. On the hangs of the Mountains, corn is ftill green; but in the lower lands, harveft is now (the twentythird of Auguft) at its height :---more than half cut, and fome carried.

The SURFACE is exceedingly broken, into fharp ridges, and deep, fteepfided vallies; efpecially on the lower declivities of the general range of hills; as between Callington and Lefkard. On the upper parts, as between Lefkard and Bodmin, the fwells are more rounded, and the vallies wider and lefs fteep.

The SOIL is very various, as to quality; but even the tops of the lower mountains are far from barren; fupporting numerous herds of cattle, as well as many fheep :--- much more productive of grafs, than the heaths of Yorkfhire; though every part produces more or lefs heath. Between

St. Ive

St. Ive and Lefkard, and below this toward the Sea, is a tract of charming land : five or six quarters of barley, an acre, are now harvefting. The *fpecies of foil* appears to be very much like that of Weft Devonfhire.

The subsoil is alfo fimilar :---namely, a flatey rock, and a kind of rufty rotten flate, or rubble.

Rivers. Several large Brooks pafs from the Mountains, fouthward, to the Sea.

Navigation. None of the Eftuaries ftretch up fo high as this road. That of Looe reaches within a few miles of Lefkard.

The roads are of ftone, and in fome parts extremely well kept. The gates few, and the tolls moderate. Toll Roads are now formed between moft or all of the market towns. The Roads of Cornwall were, formerly, very rough and dangerous; efpecially acrofs the open heaths, among the Mines ! yet, at the firft introduction of them, in this Country, obftinate riots took place.

Mines. Some, but not many, in this ride :---They are, now, I underftand, chiefly confined to the Weftern parts of the County.

The

The MANUFACTURE of the Diſtrict, I believe, is principally Woollen Yarn, for the Devonſhire Sergemakers and Clothiers.

The TOWNSHIPS appear to be large,--- with numerous Hamlets.

The PRODUCE, of the Incloſures, moſtly *Corn.* The *Heaths* ſupport the cattle in ſummer, and great part of the winter months. The principal requiſite is in courſe, Straw, to feed them with, in the depth of winter. Some *Meadows* appear in the bottoms ; but little *upland graſs* is ſeen : and but very little *Woodland*; except in the Dingles, at the heads of the vallies, next the heaths.

FUEL. Towards the Mountains, Turf (provincially " vags")and Peat (provincially " Turf.") But little of the Peat, of theſe hills, is firm enough, it ſeems, to be charred (as on Dartmore), for the uſe of Black-ſmiths.

INCLOSURES. The Mountains and their ſkirts are open :---the lower lands all in-cloſed.

The FIELDS are well ſized, and well formed.

FENCES:

Fences. The banks thinner and lower, than in Weſt Devonſhire ; but of the ſame form.

The Buildings are moſtly of Stone and Slate : ſome " Cob"—or Mudwall.

Crops. Wheat and Barley, with ſome Oats and Turneps (unhoed), with a little Clover and upland Ley. But not a Bean nor a Pea (unleſs harveſted), in this Ride !

The cattle are of the Weſt of England breed : bred and kept on the heaths, in great numbers, from yearlings to aged Oxen : working theſe occaſionally from the heath !

The Sheep of the heaths are tall, and ill formed : ſome polled, ſome horned : yet, apparently, all of the ſame old ſtock : the Ewes are now at rut : the Rams have moſtly large horns.

Beasts of labor. Some Oxen and Horſes in carriages. But Packhorſes ſeem ſtill to be much in uſe.

Implements. A ſingular kind of two-wheel carriage, for Horſes or Oxen, is here in common uſe ; eſpecially, I believe, to carry harveſt produce upon. It is called

B 4   a " wain;"

a " WAIN ;" and it is a hay cart, or wain, without fides : having only two arches bending over the wheels, to keep the load from bearing upon them ! with a wince behind. How fimple ; and, being low, how eafily loaded ! I met two on the road, laden with wool ; each, with two oxen at the pole, and two horfes before them.

MANURE. Lime and Beat afhes are univerfal. A confiderable portion of the country is now fet with roof heaps of Lime, and with velled Beat, now burning. A great quantity of earth, I fee, is burnt. All, no doubt, for Wheat. Theorifts I find are, here, againft burning the *foil* ; but Farmers, to a man, I underftand, are for it.

The TILLAGE is apparently better, here, than in Devonfhire. About Lefkard, the land appears to be in a good ftate of culti-vation.

ORCHARDS evidently diminifh, with the diftance Weftward.

WOODLANDS.—Very few : fome diftant Oak coppice.—Peeling on the ftub extends into Cornwall.

ORNA-

ORNAMENT. The views are frequently picturable, and sometimes grand : but they cloy, through a frequency of repetition, and a degree of famenefs.

HARVESTING. Bufy " handreaping :" faw feveral *women* at work. Make fhocks of ten fheaves : nine in a fquare, and one as a hood, as in Devonfhire. But, unlefs the ftraw be long, and the hood fheaf be made large and ftraight, the covering is incompleat. Mow chiefly with bows; but cradles, I fee, are to be fold. About Bodmin, the Wheat in general feems to be made into " *arrifh mows*," or field ftacklets, of about a load each.

FURZE. There are two diftinct fpecies, or varieties, now in full blow. The lower fkirts of the uncultivated hills are gilded with them. One of them is the creeping fort, which is common to the Southern Counties; the other is called the " French Furze;" and Taviftock, I underftand, has long been a market for Furze feed.

The GENERAL STATE OF HUSBANDRY, in fome parts of this ride, is above mediocrity; except in the culture of Turneps.

Between

Between St. Ive and Lefkard, is a paffage of as well cultivated land, as moft in the kingdom.

Towns. *Callington*, is a fmall market town ; and a *borough*. *Lefkard* is a large, populous, decent-looking place, and would appear refpectable in any part of the King-dom. It is likewife a *borough*. *Bodmin*, though one of the County towns, is much inferior, in fize and refpectability. This, too, is a *borough*.

BODMIN to BUCKLAND.

THE elevation of the Country is very great, between Bodmin and Five Lanes, over Bodmin Down, and Temple Moor. Some very high points of view are reached. Saw the cliff and the eftuary of Padftow. In a clear day, both feas are obfervable (near Fowey and Padftow). Some re-markable rugged mountains are feen towards the North coaft. Paffed "Dofmary Pool," a fmall lakelet, about a mile in circum-ference, upon the higher part of thefe heaths ;

heaths; and croffed a quaking bog; which has formerly, no doubt, been a lake. From the elevations furmounted in this ride, and from the top of the caftle of Launcefton, perhaps half of Cornwall, and a very large portion of Devonfhire, are feen over: the whole a ftrongly featured country.

CLIMATURE. Some Wheat *upon* the hills is ftill quite green. The harveft, in this elevated fituation, is in general very late. Sometimes, being prolonged, till after Michaelmas *.

SURFACE. About ten miles of the upper part of the heaths, over which this road paffes, is tamely billowy; the fwells refembling thofe of the Downs of the Southern Counties; with lofty mountains on each hand; a charming ride, *in fine weather.* The remaining ten miles, to Launcefton, and from thence to Buckland, is the fame abruptly broken country, which prevails throughout the more cultivated parts of the two Counties.

The

* An intelligent fellow traveller; formerly of Bodmin: now of Launcefton.

The soil towards Bodmin is of a mean
quality ; neverthelefs, the Downs and
Moors are thickly ftocked with Cattle and
Sheep; efpecially with the former : faw,
on one of the higher knolls, fome hundreds
in a herd !

About Launcefton, are fome wellfoiled,
but very fteep hills. At Milton *Abbots!*
is a plot of the fineft grafsland in the Kingdom ! Grazing ground of a very fuperior
quality. The Midland Counties cannot
fhew better. Alfo about Lamerton and
Taviftock, is fome good grazing land.

MINES. There is no " mine" within
fight of this ride. But two or three confiderable " ftream works" are feen : one of
which I ftopt to look into. In a ftream
work, there is no " lode" or body of ore ;
the tin being lodged in fmall particles or
fragments, among the earth (at two or three
to twenty or thirty feet deep) which is
wafhed by a rill or ftream, cofiveyed, by
art, to the required fpot * ; the metal and
ftones remaining ; while the foil is carried
away

* Query, Have STREAM WORKS given rife to "LEATS,"
or made Streams, in this Country ?

away with the ftream: thus annihilating the *land,* in the moft compleat manner ingenuity could devife.

RIVERS. The Tamer and Tavey: alfo the heads of fome of the Southern rivers.

The ROAD in general is good. For a confiderable way, the ftones are covered with a kind of rough fand, or fmall gravel, apparently, the loofe materials of which granite is compofed; making an admirable road.

INCLOSURE.—The moors are open: except fome finall inclofures, about Temple &c. Cultivated lands are everywhere inclofed.

PRODUCE—as before.

MANUFACTURE.—Yarn.

BUILDINGS. — Stone and Slate. At Launcefton the houfes are moftly faced with Slates: fome of them three or four feet fquare. The Church is of Moorftone, deeply and richly fculptured! Subftantial, and beautiful, as a Gothic building: the workmanfhip muft have been immenfely great; feeing the hardnefs of the materials —a fhining granite.

FIELDS

FIELDS—as before.

FENCES—increaſe toward Devonſhire, ſwelling to their fulleſt magnitude, at Buckland Place.

CROPS—as before; excepting the grazing grounds of Milton and Taviſtock.

CATTLE. The Moor ſtock are of the Weſt of England breed: ſaw ſome oxen which would fat to ſixty or ſeventy ſtone on theſe heathy mountains! All in very good ſtore condition.

SHEEP. The ſame tall, aukward ſort, as about Bodmin.

GOATS. Saw ſeveral browzing on furze. I was told that numbers are kept in Cornwall, for milking; ſome herds conſiſting of a hundred head; and that Goats' and Kids fleſh are not uncommon in the Corniſh markets.

BEAST OF LABOR—as above.

MANURE. Beat aſhes, and " ſea ſand;" a fine *ſhell marl*; which is brought in great quantities from the North coaſt, by the Padſtow river, to within three miles of Bodmin; and carried, by land, many miles.

TILLAGE—as before.

HAR-

HARVESTING—the fame.

STATE OF HUSBANDRY,—much the fame :—fomewhat inferior.

ORCHARDS—increafe toward Devon-fhire.

WOODLANDS. There are few in Corn-wall; except on the banks of the Tamer.

ORNAMENT. The mountain views are extenfive and grand : thofe from the lower points are frequently picturefque.

TOWNS. *Temple*, a DESERTED VIL-LAGE! The only one I have ever feen. Some years ago, not a fingle perfon lived in the townfhip! (a Curacy appendant to Blifland) and only one little farmhoufe is now inhabited:——the ruins of half a dozen more ; the body of the Church down ; the Chancel remains. GOLDSMITH, furely, muft have travelled this road!

Launcefton—provincially and univerfally, throughout the country, "*Laanfon*," is a genteel looking place ; but aukwardly fitu-ated ; on the brink and fide of a very fteep hill. The ftreet leading to Newport is as fteep, almoft, as the roof of a houfe. The caftle, which has been a very ftrong fortrefs,

com-

commands some charming views. *New-port* a paltry *borough:*—a mean looking hamlet; belonging to the parish of St. Stephen's, a village which stands opposite to Launceston. *Milton Abbots* a charming situation. The Abbots were admirable judges of soils and situations. *Tavistock* is also well situated; and was heretofore famous for its *abbotry.*

GENERAL OBSERVATIONS. I am agreeably disappointed with respect to Cornwall. From what I had seen on the banks of the Tamer*, I expected to have found, as I went farther Westward, a wretched country, wretched roads, wretched towns, wretched accommodations, and wretched inhabitants. On the contrary, the country, whether in point of soil or cultivation,—except the higher mountains, and they are good in their kind,—is above mediocrity. The roads, their unlevelness apart, are among the best in the kingdom. The towns, substantial and neat. The accommodations, equal to anything met with, out of the great roads. The inhabitants, intelligent, civil, are said to be extremely hospitable,

are

* See No. 3. of the following MINUTES.

are affable, clean in their appearance, and handſome in their perſons. What moſt diſguſts a ſtranger, in travelling through Cornwall, is the inordinate number of its boroughs; and this impropriety lies not with the people of Cornwall. There are none, indeed, ſo ſenſible of it, as the inhabitants themſelves.

DARTMORE,

AND ITS

UNCULTIVATED ENVIRONS.

THE Incidents, which led me to a knowledge of this District, are various. I had repeated occasions to traverse the WESTERN SKIRTS of Dartmore. I purposely ascended the SOUTHERN HEIGHTS, to view the striking features which that side of it exhibits, and to catch a bird's eye view of the District of the South Hams. I crossed the SUMMIT, in travelling between Morton and Buckland. And I skirted the NORTH-WESTERN MARGIN, in passing between Tavistock and Okehampton. I have, therefore, had opportunities of seeing almost every square mile of

its

its furface, and of obferving its natural characters, in different and diftant parts.

The SITUATION, of this uncultivated
tract of country, is towards the Weftern
fide of Devonfhire; being, in part, feparated from the Cornifh mountains, by the
cultivated banks of the Tamer: but, to the
North of Taviftock, the fkirts of Dartmore,
and thofe of the uncultivated wilds of
Cornwall, may be faid to unite: for although they are ftiewed with plots of cultivated lands, there is no regular line of
feparation; and the fame mixed country
fpreads wide, on the North-Weft quarter,
towards Launcefton, and to the immediate
environs of Okehampton. On the South,
lies the fertile Diftrict of the South Hams;
and a continuation of the Chudleigh or
Hall Down Hills, broken in a moft ftriking
manner, feparates it on the Eaft, from the
vale of Exeter.

The EXTENT of thefe wild lands is
not eafy to eftimate; there being no deter-
minate line, on the North-Weft fide. A
circle of twenty miles diameter, would,
perhaps, comprize the whole extent of the

open

open lands, in this part of Devonſhire; excluſively of the incloſed lands, which lie
intermixed among them. Admitting this
ſuppoſition to be ſufficiently near the truth,
to give a general idea of the extent of thoſe
open lands, we may ſay that they cover more
than three hundred ſquare miles of ſurface,
—amount to more than two hundred
thouſand acres.

In ELEVATION above the ſea, theſe
lands are greatly varied. The extended
ſummit of the main body of the mountain,
is raiſed, in a ſingular manner, above the
ſurrounding country; eſpecially on the
South ſide. Looking down, even from the
midway ſtages, upon the South Hams, an
upland Diſtrict, the comparative elevation
is ſo great, as to render the idea of difficulty,
in travelling acroſs the latter, truly ridicu-
lous. Nevertheleſs, the ſea waſhing, in a
manner, the foot of the mountain, its poſitive
height is inconſiderable, compared with
that of many leſs mountain-like maſſes,
which occur in the more central parts of
the Iſland. On the North ſide, the ſtages
are lengthened, and the general deſcent

much

much lefs abrupt. The outfkirts, round Brent Tor, and towards Launcefton, form an extended flat, mean in elevation, compared with the towering heights, which overlook it, on either fide *

The SURFACE, of Dartmore proper, is truly mountainous. The compofition is grand; the lines in general lengthened, and the features large : not abrupt and broken, like the minor hills of Devonfhire. Neverthelefs, the fummits of feveral of the higher fwells of Dartmore are truly favage, and rendered finely picturefque, by reafon of immenfe piles of ftones, or huge fragments of rock, thrown confufedly together,

in

* The conical hillock of BRENT-TOR, pointed with rugged rocks, and furmounted by a Church! rifes in the center of this wide flat. From the grounds of Buckland, this hillock affumes the character of a mountain height of confiderable magnitude; and, in navigating the Sound of Plymouth, it is ufed as a landmark, at more than twenty miles diftance;—yet, in reality, it is but an inconfiderable hillock. A proof of the extreme levelnefs of this paffage of country.

LAUNCESTON CASTLE, crowning a higher, but more rotund eminence, is another ftriking feature of the fame fine, broad, favage face.

in the moft grotefque manner: fometimes crowning the knolls, but oftener hanging on their brows.

In fome parts, the furface is thickly ftrewed with ftones; which, in many inftances, appear to have been collected into piles; on the tops of prominent hillocks as if in imitation of the natural Tors:—The "*ftone burrows,*" of Dartmore, refemble the *Cairns,* of the Chiviot and Grampian hills.

The WATERS of this tract of mountain are merely the torrents, which pour down its furrowed fides, in every direction. The DART is the moft confiderable ftream that owes its fupport to thefe hills.

The SOILS of thefe unreclaimed lands are greatly above the par of mountain foils, in the Ifland at large. They are fuperior to thofe of the Highlands of Scotland, and very fuperior to thofe of the North of England. Some of the higher fwells, it is true, are covered with black moory earth; and in the dips between them, peat bogs are frequent, and dangerous, not only to ftrangers who travel the crofs roads, but to

C 4 paf-

pafturing ftock. And, in many parts, the foil is much encumbered with ftones; which, in fome, occupies, perhaps, half the furface. Neverthelefs, there are extenfive tracts, even of the upper grounds, that enjoy a loamy foil, nearly free from ftones, and of a fufficient depth for cultivation : wanting nothing but a genial climature, and a proper fupply of manure, to render them valuable, as arable lands. And foils of ftill better quality are obfervable, on fome of the marginal Commons; though, on others, thofe of inferior value may be found.

The SUBSOILS are equally various. I have obferved a ftoney rubble, or foul YELLOW GRAVEL, refembling that of the Yorkfhire mountains; alfo a friable, BROWN ROCK; and, even on the higher hills, LOAM, of a fufficient depth for every purpofe of land.

The PRESENT PRODUCTION of Dartmore and its uncultivated environs may with fome little licence be faid to be HERB-AGE!—greenfward! even of the higheft bleakeft hills; frequently intermixed, however, with HEATH; which, indeed, chiefly

occupies

occupies the worſt-foiled parts of the mountain; while, on the lower grounds, the
FURZE, particularly the trailing' ſort, is
prevalent. There is little if any WOOD, I
believe, on the unappropriated parts of this
traƈt of country: the FUEL, uſed by the
bordering inhabitants, being the produce
of the peat-bogs, and the black moory
foils; as in other mountainous Diſtriƈts *.

The APPLICATION of the paſturable
produce, which this uncultivated wild at
preſent throws out, is to CATTLE, SHEEP,
and HORSES, and ſome few RABBITS.

The RIGHT of DEPASTURE belongs
to different intereſts. A confiderable part
of the mountain is FOREST LAND, ſubjeƈt
to the ſuperiority of the DUCHY OF CORN-
WALL. The outſkirts, and parts of the
hills, are appendant to the MANORS of the
ſubjoining country; and the right of paſturage veſted in the appropriated lands of
thoſe manors. And befide this intrinſic
right,

* Some of the PEAT is of a ſuperior quality; admitting of being CHARRED; and in this ſtate, it is uſed by
BLACKSMITHS, inſtead of pit coal.

right, over their respective commons, many of those lands have a prescriptive right, on the forest, by paying an inconsiderable sum —a few pence—annually, under the name of *Venville money*, to the Duchy. The Duchy, neverthelefs, preferves the right of stocking the forest lands, by *agiftment*: and stock are sent, in numbers, from distant townships; paying a very low price for their pasturage: not more than a shilling or eighteen pence, a head, being paid for the summer's run of cattle!

Beside the CATTLE thus brought together by agiftment, great numbers are reared, by the Venville tenants, on the verge of the forest; under a routine of practice that has been already mentioned *.

The SHEEP, being drawn together, from various quarters, differ as to breed. On the Southern hangs, and on the upper parts of the mountain, the polled breed of the South Hams are mostly seen. But, on the Northern and Western sides of it, the partially horned breed, which has been
no-

* See Vol. I. P. 244.

noticed *, are prevalent; correfponding, in general appearance, with the eftablifhed breed of the Cornifh mountains; but of a better frame. In winter, thofe fheep are drawn down to the inclofed country, where the ewes drop their lambs, and return with them, in the fpring, to their mountain pafture.

Hence, the leading OBJECT of the MOORSIDE FARMER is to raife fodder enough for his cattle, and to preferve grafs enough for his fheep, to fupply them, during the winter months; depending, almoft wholly, on the commonable lands, for their fummer maintenance; his milking cows and rearing calves excepted: working oxen are, everywhere, feen on the commonable land, both of Devonfhire and Cornwall: their work, under this treatment, being in courfe moderate.

The PRESENT VALUE of thefe lands appears, from this general view of their application, to be far from inconfiderable. I had not an opportunity of eftimating the aggregate

---

* See Vol. I. P. 259.

aggregate of the flock they fupport. But
an eye, accuftomed to obfervations of this
nature, may readily difcover, that, in a
POLITICAL LIGHT, thefe uncultivated
lands are, at prefent, of fome eftimation.
For admitting that a Moorfide Farmer, by
the affiftance of thefe lands, in fupporting
his ftock nine or ten months of the year,
is enabled to rear, and forward to market,
twice the number of cattle and fheep (or
even one fourth of fuch additional number),
that he could without their affiftance,—
the aggregate increafe of produce to the
community, would be found, on calculation, to be worthy of public regard.
And, in a PRIVATE point of view, if one
may judge from the good eftimation in
which Venville farms are held,—from the
extraordinary prices which the Moorfide
men give for rearing calves,—namely, fifteen to twentyfive fhillings, at three days
old ! a price which they nowhere elfe bear,
—and from the comfortable livelihoods
which the fmalleft of thefe farmers are
enabled to make,—thefe lands are not, at
prefent, wholly thrown away.

Never-

Neverthelefs, though they are doubtlefs of confiderable value, at prefent, it does not follow that they are, at prefent, in their moft valuable ftate.

To fpeak, in pofitive terms, of the means requifite to the

IMPROVEMENT

of this uncultivated tract of country, might be prefumptuous, in one who has confef-fedly given it only a curfory incidental examination. But it has alfo been pre-mifed, that the paffage of country, under confideration, is of a fpecies fimilar to the Moors of Yorkfhire, and the Mountains of Perthfhire,—both of which I have examined with attention, and have, at different periods of time, feparately digefted my ideas, with refpect to their improvement: cir-cumftances which enable me to fpeak, with greater confidence, on the improvement of the moory mountains of Devonfhire; whofe diftinguifhing characteriftics lie, chiefly, in the fuperiority of foil and climature, com-pared with thofe of the unreclaimed lands of Yorkfhire and Perthfhire.

In

In suggesting hints for the improvement
of Dartmore and its uncultivated environs,
it will be proper to consider the mountain
or forest lands, separately from the commons,
and lower grounds of the extensive flat
which has been mentioned; as they appear
to me to require somewhat different principles of improvement.

In the improvement of the HIGHER
LANDS, the leading objects appear, to me,
to be wood and herbage. Their *climature*, I apprehend, unfits them for the
profitable production of corn : and a
want of *manure* is another bar to this species
of produce. Neverthelefs, there may be
dips and unreclaimed vallies, which, *as
limited home grounds*, might admit of a
courfe of arable management.

But fpeaking generally of thefe lands,
the firft means of improvement appears to
me, to be that of planting, or otherwife
covering with wood, the stoney surfaces: not more to encreafe the value of
thefe particular parts, than to improve the
climature of the whole. The *Birch*, the
Mountain Sorb, and the *Larch*, if judicioufly
pro-

propagated, would flourish, I apprehend, on the bleakest exposures.

To improve the HERBAGE of the freer surface of these exposed lands, various means might be suggested.

Running high FENCE MOUNDS across the current of the Southwest winds, and planting them with Birch, Mountain Sorb, Elder, Holly, Furze, Broom, &c. in the Devonshire manner; but making the top of the mound hollow, or concave, to collect and retain moisture, and to skreen the young plants, or seedlings, in their tender state. It were impossible, perhaps, to conceive a better fence, for bleak mountain lands, than the ordinary hedge of Devonshire. The mound is an immediate fence and shelter; and the coppice wood, as it grew up, could not fail, from its relative height above the subjoining lands, to IMPROVE their CLIMATURE; and encourage, in a particular manner, the *growth of herbage*; beside being, at the same time, singularly friendly to pasturing stock. The only doubt, as to the propriety of raising such fences, across the bleak lands of Dartmore,

more, lies in the expence of doing it: for, great as the pofitive advantages would noubtlefs be found,—if the expence of raifing them overbalanced thefe advantages, fuch means of improvement would be altogether ineligible to be profecuted, by *Individuals*, however profitable the effect might be to the *Public*. The freer, better-foiled parts of Dartmore, I am of opinion, would pay Individuals, amply, for this CARDINAL IMPROVEMENT.

To change the prefent produce to more profitable pafturage, either in the open or an inclofed ftate, different means might be purfued.

BURNING OFF THE HEATH of the black moory parts, and pafturing them hard with fheep, would tend to extirpate the heath, and bring up herbage in its place. The Cheviot hills of Northumberland, and fimilar hills in the South of Scotland, were probably brought to their prefent ftate of green turf, by this means.

SODBURNING the more loamy foils, fowing RAPE AND GRASS SEEDS, and FOLDING OFF THE PRODUCE, with fheep, would

would be a ready means of meliorating the herbage.

If, by the intervention of Hedge mounds, the climature of thefe Hills could be rendered fufficiently genial for the maturation of RAPE SEED, and fhould their foils be found fufficiently productive of this valuable crop, the propriety of erecting fuch fences would no longer remain doubtful; as a full crop of this grain would amply repay any reafonable expence that could be incurred by inclofing; and the inclofure would amply recompenfe the lofs, which the foil could fuftain, from the exhauftion of *one grain crop:* grafs feeds being, in courfe, fown with the rape feed, or over the plants in the fpring; or a due portion, at either feafon.

By DRAINING the fpringy flopes of hills, and perhaps fome of the Peatbogs, the produce of thofe parts might be very materially improved.

By WATERING, fuch parts of the lower flopes as can command water, the herbage, perhaps, might be effentially bettered.

VOL. II.   D   But

But very much would depend on the quality of the water; and this experience would readily prove.

By MANURING, fomething might doubt-lefs be done, towards the melioration of the herbage. The vegetable mold of the Peatbogs, either in a crude recent ftate, or in the ftate of charcoal, or in that of afhes, would, with moral certainty, be found ferviceable to the loamy foils. And earthy fubftances, which, if fought for, might doubtlefs be found, could not fail of pro-ducing beneficial effects, on the black moory lands. It is needlefs to add, that if Lime could be brought to thefe lands, at a mo-derate expence, there would be little rifque in the free ufe of it. With its powerful aid, even CORN might be produced, on many of the lands under notice; but whe-ther with *eventual* advantage, either to the Proprietor or the Public (unlefs on a fmall fcale), is a matter of great uncertainty.

The moft profitable STOCK for thefe lands, in the ftate of improvement above fuggefted, would probably be found to be *young* Cattle, *Sheep*, and *Rabbits*.

There

There appears to be many fituations in which the laft would be moft eligible. Seeing the local fituation of thefe weak-foiled lands, --- between the markets of Exeter and Plymouth,---and the favorable turn of furface, which Nature has given to many of them, for the propagation of this fpecies of farm ftock, it is rather extraordinary that RABBIT WARRENS fhould not be more common, in this Diftrict, than they appear to be at prefent. But, perhaps, the true reafon has been already affigned. See Vol. I. Page 271.

In the improvement of the LOWER GROUNDS of this extenfive tract of unreclaimed lands,

CLIMATURE is the firft object of attention. It is well known, to thofe who have embraced opportunities of obferving natural effects, that the Climature of an extended and naked plain is frequently more fevere and chilling, both to the animal and the vegetable creation, than that of a billowy furface, of much greater elevation. The wind, in paffing over the latter, is broken into eddies, and its effects are thereby

foftened:

foftened: befide, let the blaft blow from
whence it may, fome part of fuch a furface
will always afford a degree of fhelter, to
animals that have free range over it; and
even vegetables, that are fixed, enjoy by
turns, as the wind fhifts, the advantages of
its fhelter---while, over an extent of naked
level furface, the current rufhes forward
with unabating force; and let it fet from
whatever quarter, vegetables and animals
are equally expofed to its unrelenting fe-
verity. Some Oaks, fcattered over the
flat of wild lands now under confideration,
might be adduced, with numberlefs other
facts, in evidence of the truth of this theory.
They are cut down flat, as with an edge-
tool. Had they ftood on the heights of
Maker, expofed to the immediate fea blaft,
they would not probably have fuffered more.

Hence, in this fituation, as on the hills,
the firft ftep towards improvement would
be to convert to WOODLAND, fuch parts as
are unfit for cultivation; and to raife
COPPICE HEDGES acrofs the line of the
moft mifchievous winds, as fkreens to the
culturable lands.

In

In a Climature thus improved, and with a fufficient fupply of LIME, at a moderate price, I am of opinion that fome confiderable proportion of thefe flat lands might be fubjeded, with profit, to a courfe of arable Management. But without a plentiful fupply of Lime, or other calcareous MANURE, it appears to me more than probable, from what I have feen of thefe lands, that very few of them would pay for cultivation, as arable lands.

I am therefore of opinion, that, without the affiftance of INLAND NAVIGATION, this extenfive tract of Country muft necef-farily remain in its prefent ftate, or be im-proved as pafture grounds, in the manner which has been already fuggefted, for the higher lands of Dartmore.

Viewing this wide extent of Country, which, with moral certainty, might be highly improved, by means of a plentiful fupply of LIME; Viewing, next, the numerous tracts of uncultivated lands be-tween Okehampton and Biddeford, which are evidently ftill more improveable, as will prefently be fhewn, and by the fame

MANURE:

MANURE :---And, laftly, viewing the extenfive tracts of Woodland, feen in paffing
between the places laft mentioned, and the
value of SHIP TIMBER at Plymouth,---
there can be little rifque in faying, that
there is no other Diftrict in this Ifland in
which the LANDED INTEREST calls equally
loud for Inland Navigation, as the line of
Country between PLYMOUTH and BIDDE-
FORD.

And feeing, at the fame time, the length,
and ftill more the uncertainty, of the
paffage, between Wales and the port of
Plymouth, by fea; and the quantity of
CULM which is now ufed for burning Lime,
on the banks of the various Eftuaries that
branch out of it, as well as COALS for the
ufe of Plymouth and its neighbourhood,---
it appears that the INTERESTS of TRAFFIC
are alfo concerned.

Finally, admitting, what I believe is
known to be a fact, that it is the bulky
articles, here particularized --- namely,
LIME, COALS, and TIMBER, not the Boxes
and Bales of Trade, that render Inland
Navigation profitable,--- it may be fairly
concluded,

concluded, that no Line of Canal is more likely to *pay*, than that now under con-fideration.

The proper direction, of the Southern part of the Line, is evident. The TIDE flows within the Eftuary or Mouth of the TAVEY: and, where the Tide ends, the CANAL fhould commence; winding up the valley of the Tavey, to TAVISTOCK; a branch being thrown off, up the valley of the Walkham, to HARROW BRIDGE, for the ufe of the extenfive Commons in that neighbourhood, and to catch the ufe of the public road which there croffes the valley. Above Taviftock, the main line would ftill wind with the valley of the Tavey, to the FOOT OF THE DARTMORE HILLS (a moft defirable point to be gained),---and thence bend acrofs the uncultivated flat, towards OKEHAMPTON.

In travelling between Taviftock and Okehampton, I obferved (between Lydford and the latter place) that the road was re-paired with LIMESTONE !---black marble; a circumftance which renders it more than probable, that the raw materials of improve-

D 4 ment

ment lie within the field to be improved; and that FUEL only would be wanted, to render the profecution eafy and profitable.

Without intending to cenfure the fupine-nefs, which has lately prevailed in this Country, with refpect to the permanent improvement of its furface, I will not hefitate to fay, that had advantages, like thofe which are here adduced, occurred within the interior of the Ifland, they would long ago have been feen and embraced: and that whenever the fpirit of enterprize, in this extreme part of it, fhall fhift its ground, from MINING to AGRICULTURE, the Improvement which is here pointed out, will be carried into effect.

DISTRICT

DISTRICT THE FOURTH.

NORTH DEVONSHIRE,

PREFATORY REMARKS.

AN accurate Definition of what is familiarly called "NORTH DEVON," or "the North Country," I fhall not attempt to give. It is generally applied, I believe, to the Country lying towards the North Coaft; round Biddeford, Barnftaple, and South Moulton. But the Diftrict to which this name aptly applies, is fituated between the Mountain of Dartmore and the Sea;--- comprizing a wide extent of Country: diverfified, it is true, in foil and furface; but it has no diftinct feparation of parts, large enough to warrant its being divided into feparate Diftricts.

As the only opportunity I had of collecting information, refpecting this Diftrict,

was

was obtained by an EXCURSION, undertaken for the purpofe of viewing its prominent features, and of remarking the overt
practices, which meet the eye of every
Traveller, who looks attentively round
him, --- I will not attempt a digefted
Regifter, either of the Diftrict, or its Rural
Management; but offer a Tranfcript of my
Travelling Journal *.

The route which I thought it proper to
take, was from OKEHAMPTON to HA-
THERLEY, TORRINGTON, BIDDEFORD,
BARNSTAPLE, SOUTH MOULTON, and
acrofs the Country to DULVERTON (to
catch

* It is, however, with diffidence and fome reluctance,
I adopt this mode of publication. And I have only to
fay, in its behalf, that the feries of remarks, which are
here publifhed, arofe from facts and reflections, that
occurred, in paffing through the Diftrict under review;
and were in general *dictated*, while the feveral fubjects of
Remark—remained under the eye.

The defective ftyle, in which they appear, is the convenient one of a Journal,—or *verbal fketch book*. it is
concife; and the pronoun, or the verb, which may frequently be wanting, is readily to be *underftood*. If the
firft perfon were ufed, egotifm would difguft: if the
fecond (as it is in the ordinary ftyle of Journals) fenfe
would be facrificed.

catch a view of Exmoor and the fine
fcenery of its Environs) ; and thence, to
BAMPTON and TIVERTON.

OKEHAMPTON

AND ITS

ENVIRONS.

SUNDAY 14 SEPTEMPER, 1794.

THE TOWN, well fized and refpectable, confidering the reclufenefs of its
fituation, is feated in a deep bafon, broken
into three parts, by the narrow wooded
vallies of the Oke and its two principal
branches : the former winding towards the
North, the latter fpreading wide to the
Eaft and Weft; and embracing, as with
arms, the Northern point of the Dartmore
Mountain ; which here forms a flattened
ftage, of confiderable extent and elevation ;
overlooking the town, and forming one fide
of the bafon in which it is fituated. The
face of the fteep is finely hung with wood ;
—moftly large full-headed Oaks ; being

part

part of the ancient demefne lands, belonging to the Caftle of Okehampton ; whofe
ruins ftill occupy a peninfular hillock that
faces this bold woody fteep ; being divided
from it by the Weftern branch of the Oke,
The fcenery truly alpine.

Sheep, of a diminutive fize, are grazing
among the ruins of the Caftle. Various in
head, as thofe of Weft Devonfhire and
Cornwall. Some of them refembling very
much, in head and carcafe, the fize apart,
the improved breed of Dorfetfhire.

The fite of the Caftle, and the fteep rugged height, on the face of which it ftood,
appears to be compofed of flatey rock,
fimilar to that of Weft and South Devonfhire.

Upon this eminence, and on the Weftern
brink of the Bafon, ftands the principal
Church of Okehampton : proudly fituated ;
and forming a good objeét from the oppofite height ; making one feature of a fine
landfcape.

The entire Environs, and the views
from them are rich and beautiful ; but the
fcale is fmall. A truly monaftic fituation ;
---rich

—rich and reclufe---yet, I believe, without the veftige of a monaftery!

The fertile fwells are now loaded with grafs; and fome of them ftocked with good Cows, of the North Devonfhire breed. But little corn; and moft of this is ftill in the field. The North fide of a Mountain Diftrict is naturally liable to a backwardnefs of climature.

OKEHAMPTON

TO

TORRINGTON.

(17 Miles)

MONDAY 15 SEPTEMBER, 1794.

ASCEND, by a fteep ill conducted road, the Weftern banks of the Oke, and leave the cultivated Environs, at one mile from the Town.

Delightful morning!

The Okehampton hounds are gone out, towards the hills of Dartmore, another pack

now

now pafs the carriage, towards the oppofite hills.   A finely wild fporting country.

Enter an extenfive furze-grown Common ; apparently well foiled, and the fub-foil rotten flate.   Land fit for almoft any purpofe of Hufbandry.

Several plots of this Common are now fodburnt and liming for Wheat !   The entire Common lies in narrow ridges, as if it had undergone the fame operation, and been fuffered to lay down again to reft, after one crop of corn had been thus taken.

The Stock, now on this ill applied tract, are fmall Sheep; fimilar to thofe near Okehampton.

A rich Valley opens to the right : to the left a mixed Country;   marked by the Church of Ingerley : a pleafing though gayly coloured object.   But the morning is fine ; and Nature herfelf appearing gay, a white wafhed fteeple affimilates with the fcene.

Enter an inclofed, but rough, upland Country.

Farm houfes and Cottages mean : moftly of mud and thatch.

Hedgemounds

Hedgemounds in the manner of West Devonshire; but not, in general, so high.

See red soil, in the valley to the right.

More furze-covered Commons;—highly improveable: a waste of property to suffer them to remain in their present unproductive state. A patch of Wheat stubble on one of these Commons, discovers, in its own strength, that of the land.

Some rubbishly ill bred Cattle, on these Commons. The natural produce of commonable lands.

Cross a cold clayey Dip; and enter more extensive Commons. Thousands of acres of dwarf furze, which ought to be supplanted by Wheat, Beans, and Clover.

Some Timber Trees seen scattered over the Inclosures.

Grass Inclosures velled for Wheat; as in the South of Devonshire.

The spring and the autumn furzes are here intermixed, as in Cornwall and West Devonshire.

A billowy, wooded, Kentish view opens to the left.

A newly

A newly planted Hedgemound. The plants as thick as the arm, and cut down to two or three feet high, as in Weſt Devon-ſhire. The Hedgewoods Birch, Hazel, Aſh.

Enter a cold-ſoiled Woodland Diſtrict. Inſtance of Scotch Firs planted on this cold retentive ſoil!

Still more extenſive tracts of dwarf furze: Not only the Commons, but ſome Incloſures, are cropped with this unprofitable plant; the whole of theſe furze grounds lying in narrow Wheat ridges.

The common Sheep, here, are ſmall and moſtly polled.

A large parcel of hewn Timber, fit for Ship Building, collected by the ſide of the road.

The ſubſoil of theſe Commons is a red clayey gravel.

Enter an incloſed, red ſoiled plot of Country,—the immediate Environs of

HATHERLY: a mean market Town: moſtly or wholly built with red earth and thatch. Some of the houſes white-waſhed, others

others rough-caft. Obferved Reed in fheaves ; as in the Weftern parts of the County.

A beautifully wooded Dip breaks, to the left : the valley of the Torridge.

Leave fhe red foil, about a mile from Hatherly. The fubfoil a deep grouty rubble : red as oker.

Enter a cold, vale Country. The fubfoil a pale coloured clay.

A narrow flat of river-formed land.

Buildings entirely of clay.

Four Oxen, two Horfes, two Men, and a Boy, at plow !

A fhameful fall of young Timber.

A charming broad wooded Bafon, now opens to the Weft ;---between Hatherly and Sheepwafh.

And, now, a wide flat of Marfhes to the right ; apparently in a wild, negleƈted, un-produƈtive ftate.

Hewifh, Sir James Notcliff's, appears on the oppofite banks of thefe marfh lands.

A bad Turnpike road traces a high ridge of cold white clay,---commanding a ftrongly featured country.

VOL. II.　　　E　　　　Ridges

Ridges of Lime and Earth, for Wheat, are common in the adjoining Inclosures.

Coppice Hedges univerfal.

Defcend, by a fteep road, into a well foiled Dip of Land. The fubfoil flatey rubble, or rotten flate rock.

Very few Orchard Grounds in this Country.

Afcend " Padftow" Hill : an infulated eminence ; commanding a fine circle of views. To the South, the Mountain of Dartmore rifing bold to the view, and forming a remarkably ftrong feature from this point. To the Eaft, the rifing banks of the Oke and the Taw; apparently, well foiled, and well cultivated ; the foreground of this view, the Valley of " Marland"--- or Marfhland, in a ftate of neglect,---much of it occupied by furze ; to appearance, highly improveable. To the North, a ridge of well foiled arable upland. To the Weft, a well wooded Diftrict.

A delightful morning : with the Lark in full fong :---and with hounds in full cry !

A diftant view of the North Country, now begins to open.

The

The Country, here, wholly inclofed: moftly in large fquare *Devonfhire* Fields.

Paffed the firft Cart : drawn in the Cleveland manner ! three horfes ; one in the fhafts, the other two abreaft, and guided by reins : loaded with bark, for the port of Biddeford ; to be there fhipped for Ireland.

Crofs a well timbered Hollow. Much valuable Ship Timber, in this Diftrict.

Clofe woody lanes,---how tantalizing to a Traveller !

Enter a well foiled paffage ; moftly arable. Some patches of Turneps and Clover.

Very few Field Potatoes in this Diftrict.

A Box : Winfcot : the firft *Houfe* I have paffed, in this ftage.

Still a well foiled arable Country. Farms feemingly of good fize ; and not ill cultivated.

Obferve feveral good Horfes. Q. Bred in this Diftrict ?

Another paffage of good upland Country. Skirted by a cold rufhy bottom.

Meet

Meet a ftring of Lime Horfes, from Biddeford; eight or ten miles.

Lime, here, a prevailing manure.

Hedgemounds increafe in height: this, altogether, a South-Devonfhire-like Diftrict.

An extenfive view opens to the left.

Inftance of a cropt Hedge. What a lofs to the Traveller, that the practice is not prevalent.

Large white Pigs, in a good form.

A fine view of the Valley of Torrington burfts upon the eye.

Orchard Grounds encreafe.

A charming back view of the Valley above Torrington: well formed ground, happily enriched with wood and water.

An extenfive and rich view, to the right, including the Eaftern banks of the Taw.

An inftance of limed Grafsland.

Dip down to the Bridge of Torrington.

GENERAL REMARKS.

THE Townfhips in this ftage, appear to be of the middle fize. The Churches, in general, tall and confpicuous.

Of

Of the State of Inclofure, it may be faid, that about half the lands, which fall immediately under the eye, are inclofed; the reft, in coarfe furzey Commons, capable of great improvement.

The Fields are generally well fhaped, and well fized; as in Weft and South Devonfhire.

The Fences, throughout, are fimilar to thofe in the Southern parts of the County. But the Mounds are fomewhat narrower and lower.

Woodlands extenfive. Oak the prevailing wood. Much fine Timber: much alfo in a ftate of Coppice.

The Orchard Grounds are few and fmall.

The Arable Crops appear, by the ftubbles, to be chiefly Wheat and Oats: but altogether fmall, in proportion to the Grafslands and Furze Grounds, which occupy this Line of Country; efpecially towards Okehampton.

The Climature fomewhat forwarder than about Okehampton. The crops moftly harvefted,

E 3 The

The preparations, now going on for the next year's crop of Wheat, are the very fame, here, as in the South of Devonſhire; namely, ley ground burnt and limed.

Very few Cattle, or Sheep, are ſeen in the Incloſures; which are now full of graſs.

The ſtate of Huſbandry, on the whole, is conſiderably below par.

TORRINGTON

AND ITS

ENVIRONS.

THE TOWN is proudly ſituated on the brink, and partly hanging on the brow, of the Eaſtern bank of the Oke. It is a large inland Market Town; but has no thorofare to ſupport it. There is no poſting inn, in the place! and only one chaiſe kept for hire. Neverthelefs, the Town is neat, and the people alive. Circumſtances to be accounted for, only, in the many family reſidences, which appear in its neighbourhood, and which ſeldom fail to meliorate the

manners

manners of every clafs of thofe, who fall within the fphere of their influence.

The view from the fite of the Caftle---now a Bowling Green---is uncommonly fine. A wooded amphitheatre, richly diverfified : with a lengthened bend of water in the middle ground : --- and with foxhounds in the woods !

TORRINGTON

TO

BIDDEFORD.

(Seven Miles)

MONDAY, 15 SEPTEMBER, 1794.

A well foiled Common near the Town ; ftocked with fmall neat fheep.

Pafs between well foiled Inclofures : a rich and beautiful Country.

Crofs a lovely wooded valley : thriving Oak Timber ; well thinned, and fet out.

A fmall Yorkfhire plow. The firft I have obferved in the County.

The

The furface broken, abruptly, into hill and dale: a truly Danmonian paffage.

Surmount a clean upland Country. The fubftratum brown rufty rock.

Reach the fummit of the ridge : a furze-grown wafte. A broad view of the Briftol Channel meets the eye; with extenfive land views, on either fide. On the one hand, Hartland Point is a prominent and ftriking feature; on the other, Exmore? rifes boldly to the view,

Defcend towards Biddeford.

Meet ftrings of Lime Horfes, with pack-faddles and bags of Lime. Alfo two-horfe Carts, with Lime and Sea fand.

GENERAL REMARK.

This Paffage of Country, in Soil, Surface, and apparent General Management, per-fectly refembles the South-Weftern parts of Devonfhire.

BIDDEFORD

BIDDEFORD

AND ITS

ENVIRONS.

TUESDAY, 16 SEPTEMBER, 1794.

THE Town is remarkably forbidding. Meanly built houſes (timber, brick, or mud, covered with bad ſlate or thatch), ſtuck againſt a ſteep hill. The ſtreets, of courſe, are aukward ; and moſt of them are narrow. In the vacant ſpaces between the ſtreets, immenſe piles of furze faggots riſe, in the ſhape of houſes, and make the houſes themſelves appear more like hovels than they really are.

Theſe dangerous piles of fuel are for the uſe of the pottery, for which only, I believe, this Town is celebrated: chiefly, or wholly, the coarſer kinds of earthen ware.

The Bridge of Biddeford is an extraordinary erection : a high thick wall, run

acroſs

acrofs the river or narrowed eftuary ; with Gothic gateways, here and there, to let the water pafs.

The tide out : many men employed in loading packhorfes, with fand, left in the bed of the river : and, in every vacant corner about the Town, compofts of earth, mud, afhes, &c. are feen. Shell fand is faid to be plentiful on the coaft ; but little, if any of it, is brought up this river.

On the fhore of the eftuary, oppofite to the Town, are feveral limekilns, now in full work. Numbers of packhorfes, and a few carts, loading, or waiting for loads. The ftone, chiefly, and the culm with which it is burnt, wholly, brought acrofs the chan-nel, from the coaft of Wales. The kilns fimilar to thofe of Weft Devonfhire. This lime is carried fourteen or fifteen miles ; chiefly on horfeback.

STROLL

Stroll upon the High lands, to the South and West of the Town.

The fubfoil of the fkirts of the hill, is a Slate rubble. A bafe kind of Slate is ufed as a covering.

Some charming views, from the midway ftages of this eminence. To the North, the conflux of the eftuaries of the Taw and the Oke,—backed by the cultivated hills of the coaft. To the South, a beautiful bend of the narrowing eftuary of the Oke, lofing itfelf in the winding wooded valley of that river; fkreened, on either hand, by wooded heights, and backed by wilder diftances. Each of thefe views is worthy of the pencil. The former is grand; but the latter is more picturable, as a landfcape. The home views, on every fide, are pleafing. The furface finely broken; refembling that in the environs of Bridport; but the features are larger, and the lines lefs abrupt.

The foil, of this midway of the fwell, is a fertile well coloured loam; on a pale and ftronger fubfoil.

The

The whole country is inclofed; moftly in large fields, with coppice fences—cut down by the wind: a circumftance more favorable to the admirers of natural landfcape, than to the hufbandman.

No hedgerow timber: but a few groups of trees are fcattered on the hills. The fteep banks of the Oke, are chiefly hung with coppice wood.

The farm produce chiefly grafs; with fome little corn; and moft of it ftill out!

The ftock, obfervable from this ftation, are cattle and fheep. The former in herds, as if the farms were large. The fheep are above the middle fize,—and moftly polled.

Nearer the fummit of the hill, the land is colder, and the herbage coarfe: abounding with Marfh Fleabane and other aquatic weeds. But the fummit itfelf is again dry, found, and tolerably well foiled.

A wide circle of views are feen, from an Object Houfe (in ruins) near the fummit. A very extenfive view opens to the South Eaft. But the horizon is too hazy to trace it to its fartheft diftance. To the South Weft, a ftrongly featured upland Diftrict;

large

large well turned cultivated fwells, feparated, and the face of the country diverfified, by winding wooded vallies, in the
beft ftyle of Kent or Herefordfhire ; with
tall and ftately towers of Churches fcattered
over the wide fpreading fcene.

On the upper ftages of this eminence,
and in defcending its Weftern declivity,
I obferved many young horfes ; much of
the Yorkfhire breed ; but fomewhat fhorter
and thicker.

Alfo fome good North Devonfhire cows.

BIDDEFORD MARKET.

A few fat, and fome ftore cattle ; with
three or four heifers and calves. The
heifers fomewhat fmall ; but neat ; and
with remarkably fine bags ! the moft pro-
mifing appearance of milk, that I have obferved, in the Devonfhire breed of cattle.

A few fheep, and two or three colts
(weaned foals) in halters.

The Corn Market well filled with long
two-bufhel bags ; chiefly of wheat.

The

The fhambles full of good mutton;—
with a fcanty fhow of beef.

Salmon in confiderable plenty; but no
fea fifh!

The women's market well fupplied.

Cart loads of country bread, expofed in
the market place, for fale. A market
article, this, which I have not before *obferved.*

Upon the whole, the Market of Biddeford may be fet down as very refpectable.

STROLL UPON THE RISING GROUNDS, ON THE NORTH SIDE OF THE TOWN.

Thefe grounds are feparated from the
hill on which the Town is fituated, by a
creek of marfhland, in its natural ftate, as
formed by the tide; excepting a plot of
feven or eight acres, which is now em-
banking: an operation, which, if it were
carried on, with *proper exertion,* could not
fail to pay threefold for the money expended. If the men, who are employed upon

it,

it, may be confidered as a fample of the *Laborers* of North Devon, they exceed, in idlenefs, their Countrymen of the Weft.

A low bank, thrown up acrofs thefe marfhlands, furnifhes, at once, a fafe road, and gives effect to a tide mill, fituated near one end of it.

A rich loamy foil to the very fummit of this hill: a narrow ridge.

A good view of the Bay of Barnftaple, and its finely diverfified coaft : here, a flat fhore ; there fteep lofty cliffs.

Some charming near views are feen from thefe grounds. Tapley (Mr. Cleveland's) a fine fituation, is feen with advantage.

The entire environs are ftudded with *houfes*: fome of them fubftantial; others neat. Yet ftill we find the Town itfelf a contraft to Torrington The influence even of half a fcore families is not fufficient to burnifh the appearance and manners of a fmall feaport Town, in a remote fituation.

GENERAL

General Remarks.

The climature of this Diſtrict is evidently later, than that of Weſt Devonſhire?
much of the corn, grown in it, is yet out!

There are few orchards in theſe environs.

Several carts appear; but no waggons.
Packhorſes are chiefly prevalent.

The ſtate of huſbandry is on a par, with
that of the reſt of the County, I have yet
ſeen; or ſomewhat ſuperior: a laudable
aſſiduity, in collecting and mixing manures,
is ſingularly conſpicuous.

On a general view of the Diſtrict, at this
ſeaſon, it reſembles South Devonſhire, ſo
much, with reſpect to natural characters,
and Farm Management, that, in a regiſter
of their Rural Economy, they might well be
conſidered as one and the ſame Diſtrict;
excepting an obſervable ſuperiority in the
breeds of cattle and horſes, in this part of
the County; and except a ſomewhat freer
uſe of wheel carriages, here, than in the
South Hams, and Weſt Devonſhire.

BIDDEFORD

BIDDEFORD

TO

BARNSTAPLE.

(Eight miles.)

WEDNESDAY, 17 SEPTEMBER, 1794.

ANOTHER broken billowy Diftrict: high rotund fwells, feparated by deep narrow vallies.

The materials of thefe hills appear to be chiefly rotten flate, or rufty flate-ftone rubble, fimilar to that of Weft Devonfhire and Cornwall.

Creeks of marfhland branch out of the eftuary of the Taw: the foil of thefe marfhlets is fomewhat reddifh. Now ftocked with cattle. But they are at prefent in a rough unreclaimed ftate, and appear to be highly improveable.

The road of ftone, and remarkably good.

VOL. II.   F   The

The ſtems of corn ſtacks thatched with reed.

Leave a ſweet woody dell, to the right.

A ſtuccoed barn : mud-wall plaiſtered.

A breed of remarkably tall white Pigs.

Roof heaps of lime and earth compoſt, on unbroken ſward.   Q. For Wheat?

Paſs over a well-ſoiled upland country : the ſubſtratum earthy ſlate, up to the ſoil.

A few ſtone buildings obſervable.

High mound coppice hedges, full of growth.

The timber trees, *on this ſide of the County*, .are remarkably ſhorn with the *Northweſt* wind.

The wide valley of the Taw opens to the view,—and the nature of the Country changes, from clean ſound land, to a cold aquatic ſoil : alder ſwamps, ruſhy incloſures, and rough furze grounds ; with much oak wood.   The coppices in general healthy ; but the timber much injured by the coldneſs of the ſubſtratum, and the winds from the ſea.   One wood compleatly ſtag-headed : a waſte of property to let it ſtand.

Meet ſeveral flocks of " Exmore" lambs ;

many

many hundreds; invariably horned; and, moftly, even in carcafe; on their way to the Northweft of Devonfhire, and the North of Cornwall, to their winter pafture.

An inftance of coppice wood, on a flat furface; as in Kent and Suffex: the firft inftance of it, I have obferved, in the Weft of England.

Enter on the defcent into the vale, or valley, of Barnftaple.

A large field breaft-plowed, and now burning.

Still a cold foiled, well timbered Dif-trict. Much furze-grown rough ground; which appears to be very capable of im-provement.

See a heath-covered knoll, to the right. Good cows; moftly of a dark blood-red colour.

Towards the foot of the hill, the land improves   A broad flat of meadows and marfhlands.

Good grazing cattle, in rich marfhes.

Some large houfes are feen, among the fine fcenery, on the oppofite banks of the valley.

The

The bridge of Barnftaple is fimilar to that of Biddeford.

General Remarks.

The climature improves; no corn obfervable in the field, in this ftage.

The produce—arable crops, grafs, wood, and roughets of furze, and rubbifh.

Townfhips—apparently large.

The whole Country inclofed;—moftly, in large fquare fields.

The farms apparently of a good fize.

The fences truly Danmonian.

The cattle, which appeared, are of a good fort. But not fuperior to what I expected to have feen, in this neighbourhood.

No Sheep obferved, in the inclofures :

Nor wheel carriages, on the road.

In the general ftate of hufbandry, nothing *new* ftruck me, in this paffage of country.

The moft obvious improvement, of which it appears to be capable, is that of draining, burning, and fallowing, the cold rough lands.

BARN-

BARNSTAPLE

AND ITS

ENVIRONS.

THE day inceffantly rainy, and ill calculated for pedeftrian examinations.

The Town is refpectable. The ftreets
are wider and better laid out, than thofe of
old Towns generally are. Many of the
houfes are fubftantially built of brick.
But the covering, here, is of the fame
mean-looking flate, as that which is in ufe
at Biddeford.

Leith carts and Highland fledges (or implements very much refembling them!)
are feen in the ftreets of Barnftaple.

Some fmall craft in the river, and in a
creek which wafhes one fide of the Town.
And two fmall veffels on the Stocks.

Pilton, a pleafant village, adjoins to Barnftaple.

F 3

A bold

A bold Promontory, which rifes abruptly in the center of the broad valley, above the Town,—fevering the Taw from the Brook of Pilton and its fweetly winding woody Dell,—forms a ftriking feature, among the affemblage of picturable fcenes, which the environs of Barnftaple *appear*, even through the dim medium of rain, to be capable of affording.

BARNSTAPLE

TO

SOUTH MOULTON.

(Eleven Miles.)

WEDNESDAY, 17 SEPTEMBER, 1794.

A RICH flat of meadows and marfh-lands, above the Town; nearly a mile wide: evidently formed by the tide and floods.

The Country, on either fide, picturably broken, and well wooded.

Some fine Cows now in the meadows.

Sea

Sea fand compoft is here in ufe.

Pafs through Newport, a large village.

The Buildings chiefly Earth and Thatch; but fome Brick, Stone, Slate, and Pantile, in ufe.

The breed of very tall white Pigs ftill continues.

Meet more Exmore Lambs going Weft-ward to their wintering grounds.

The day is fet in for rain; yet the appear-ance of the Country is delightful beyond defcription. Perhaps rain, as varnifh, mellows the Views.

The fubftratum, here, flatey rock; worn into hollow ways.

Lofty fwells productive to their fummits, as thofe of the South Hams.

The prevailing fubfoil, flatey rubble.

A valley opens to the left: richly foiled, well cultivated, and ftocked with fine cattle.

Some large orchards in this valley.

Clofe woody hedges, with fome timber in them.

The roads in a fhameful ftate: evidently injured by the hedges. Why is not the Law enforced? In this Country, where

wood-

woodlands abound, and where coals may be had at a reasonable rate; no serious evil could arise were all the hedges in it shorn to their mounds.

Sea sand composts are still seen by the side of the road (5 miles from "Barum").

A small waste hillock appears to the right.

The substratum—a mass of rock, broken into chequers,—and rising to the soil.

Get a broad view of the rich and beautiful VALLEY OF SWIMBRIDGE.

A large flock of Sheep appear on its base.

Instance of Oats now green as Grass! the second instance observed?

A wide view opens to the East; but is curtailed by the hazeyness of the atmosphere.

Rich grassland, to the summits of the swells.

The Valley of the Taw opens, at some distance to the right: a wooded District.

A fine back view of the Estuary and its banks: broad, but grand, and picturable.

An obvious improvement, in the line of road. The hill is crossed, when its base might be traced nearly on the level.

The

The fields in this Country, as in the South of Devonſhire, appear to be large in proportion to the Farms.

A breed of ſmall ſheep; apparently with fine wool.

Rock and flate rubble riſe to the ſoil of rich graſsland.

Grazing Cattle, on the higher hills; as in the South Hams.

Meet a pair of wheels: the firſt from Biddeford.

The road improves.

A ſweet Country; but moſt difficult to be *ſeen!* A diſtant view, at length, opens to the Eaſt.

Black Limeſtone road: tolerably good.

Philley, Lord Forteſcue's noble place, breaks at once upon the eye: a finely wooded baſon. The Timber abundant, and ſeemingly well ſet out.

A herd of young cattle, and a flock of ſheep, in the grounds about the houſe.

The Farmery large; beſpeaking a ſuitable portion of demeſne in hand.

A very

A very deep quarry of black Limeſtone. Similar, in appearance, to the Chudleigh marble: but the color is leſs bright.

This capacious quarry is not leſs than fifty feet deep. The ſtones are brought up from the lower depths on horſeback ; and the water raiſed by a horſe pump.

Paſs a ſtring of two-horſe carts, guided with reins, in the Cleveland manner ! Has a colony of Clevelanders formerly ſettled in North Devonſhire, and brought with them their carts and horſes ? See page 51.

Vile roads again: and in the neighbour-hood of a great man s reſidence ! But, per-haps, his Lordſhip's Lime Work is the principal cauſe of the evil. The color of the materials, and the ſtate in which they at preſent lie, give them every appearance of roads to Coal pits.

Still an incloſed, well ſoiled Country.

A ſtately Tower, proudly ſituated. North Moulton ?

Mount a rich well turned ſwell, and enter the Town of South Moulton.

SOUTH

SOUTH MOULTON

AND ITS

ENVIRONS.

THURSDAY, 18 SEPTEMBER, 1794.

THE TOWN, which confifts of a fpacious well built Market Place, furrounded with inferior ftreets, caps a rotund hillock, fituated among other hillocks of a fimilar nature, and wearing fimilar appearances; rich and beautiful in a fuperior degree.

The foil a rich greazy loam.

The fubfoil pale rubble, or rotten flate, or a kind of foft checkered rock.

Some wood in the vallies; but not one acre of unproductive land, to be feen, in the neighbourhood. One of the fineft farming Diftricts in the Kingdom.

Walked towards the Barton of Great Hill to view Mr. Trigg's Breed of Cattle; which is reckoned one of the firft in this neighbourhood.

bourhood. And the Diftrict of South Moulton is fpoken of as the firft, for the North Devonfhire breed.

Saw fix of his Cows. All of them good. One of them fuperior to the reft: remarkable in the carcafe; well loined, wide at the hips, and fquare in the quarters; with a fine head and bone. The horns alfo fine, and fhorter than ordinary. The color a lightifh blood-red; the reft darker, and moftly with fmokey faces. All of them low on their legs: a fize between the Gloceftershire and the Herefordshire.

The day is too tempeftuous, to keep the field: and I have already gained a fufficient idea of the North Devonfhire breed of Cattle. A farther examination might gratify; but could not inftruct: they are evidently a fuperior variety of the middle-horned breed. And are of courfe one of the firft breeds of Cattle in the Ifland.

GENERAL

GENERAL OBSERVATIONS,

ON THE COUNTRY BETWEEN BIDDEFORD AND SOUTH MOULTON, INCLUDING THEIR ENVIRONS.

IN a general view of this Line of Country, —whether we attend to the height or formation of its furface,---to its foil, its fubftrata (a fhort paffage on the Weft of Barnftaple excepted), or their prefent pro-duce ; to the ftate of inclofure, the fize or fhape of fields, or the nature of their fences, ---to the fpecies of arable crops (no trace of the bean crop or other article of pulfe now obfervable) ; or the manner of pro-ducing them (fo far as it appears at this feafon) ; or to the liveftock or animals of labor (except as above excepted*)---it fo perfectly refembles the Diftrict of South Devonfhire, that they might be conceived to have once been united ; and to have been forcibly feparated, and thrown into their

prefent

* See P. 64.

prefent fituations, by the Mountain of Dartmore, in one of Nature's convulfive paroxifms, having broken them afunder, and placed itfelf in the breach.

SOUTH MOULTON

TO

DULVERTON.

(Thirteen Miles)

THURSDAY, 18 SEPTEMBER, 1794.

AT lefs than two miles from the Town, leave its fertile Environs.

A pretty but unproductive valley to the left : alders, rufhes, and rough grounds.

Climb the fide of this valley. The fub-ftratum clofe rock, up to the foil : no intervening rubble, or other earthy fubfoil : the land lean, and the produce weak : a contraft to the neighbouring lands ; though the *foils* appear to be fimilar.

Another rainy day, with a ftorm of wind.

Meet

Meet a *drove* of cart horſes, and a ſtring of ſaddle horſes, on their way to the Fair of Barnſtaple ; the property of a Dorſetſhire Dealer.

Mount a rough furze-grown height, an extenſive Common,---and catch a broad view to the South : apparently, a cold infertile Diſtrict.

Bend to the left, from the Tiverton road; and enter narrow woody lanes, barely pervious, by a carriage.

Break out of this paſs, into other Commons; and nearly approach the heaths of Exmore ; a narrow valley only intervening.

EXMORE, in this point of view, is without feature ; appears as a flat, or at moſt, a tamely billowy heath. : Its hills ſcarcely riſe above the cultivated ſwells that environ them.   This ſide of it, at leaſt, has not a trait of the Mountain character.

Wind along the brink of the valley. The oppoſite banks apparently well ſoiled and well cultivated ; though they form the immediate ſkirts or margin of the Moor.

Some wooded Dells branch out of the valley.

Sheep

Sheep on thefe Commons, fimilar to thofe of Weft Devonfhire and Cornwall! part horned; part hornlefs.

See corn in arrifh mows; or fmall field ftacks.

Trace a ridge of cold land: a woodland foil; and leave a fimilar dip to the right.

Enter and fkirt a wide fern-grown Common: large plots of fern now in fwath. Alfo dwarf furze, and fome heath. The foil deep and culturable.

Approach ftill nearer the Exmore Heaths: now crimfoned with bloffoms; which brighten as the day clears up.

The foil of the Moor Skirts fomewhat red.

Laid out in large fquare Danmonian Fields. Much of it in a ftate of arable land: a few Turneps.

The valley widens, and breaks into well foiled hillocks. The two parifhes of Eaft and Weft Anftey appear to be in a good ftate of culture. Several plowed fields; apparently clean fallows.

Meet ftrings of Lime Horfes; from Bampton Lime Works.

Several

Several inftances of good young Cattle, of the North Devon Breed.

Building Materials---Earth and Thatch: an entire fuite of new Farm Buildings, juft finifhed, of thefe materials.

Lofe fight of the Exmore Hills; but ftill keep the brink of the valley; having en-joyed a tolerably level road for feven or eight miles!

Holly abounds in this cold fituation: it is feen to mix frequently with the Alder.

Leave the high ground, and defcend into the valley. Subfoil flatey rubble.

Stirring Wheat Fallows, with four oxen: the firft oxen, and the firft plow, I have *feen* at work, in North Devonfhire!

Narrow Wheat ridges, as in Weft Devonfhire.

The road, of black Limeftone, is narrow but well laid out,

Thick polled Sheep, as in the South Hams.

Inftance of watering Grafsland: the firft I have *obferved*, in North Devonfhire.

" Dunftone," and good Grafsland, as about Moulton.

A Lime kiln : black ſtone, lodged among "Dunſtone."

Some tolerably large Orchards; with low *Devonſhire* trees; though within the *County* of Somerſet.

Another Sea, or rather Bay, of rich Danmonian ſwells.

Approach DULVERTON; by another Gothic bridge.

DULVERTON

AND ITS

ENVIRONS.

THIS ſmall Market Town is ſituated in a deep narrow valley; chiefly near its baſe, but ſomewhat climbing up its Eaſtern bank. The Church conſpicuous and neat; and the place altogether, has a plain, neat, and pleaſing appearance: and immediately below the Town is a ſmall place, Pickſton, belonging to the Ackland family.

The approach from Moulton is ſingularly ſtriking. Pickſton, a plain dreſſed place,

firſt

firſt meets the eye; and immediately the Town, equally unſuſpected, burſts abruptly into the ſequeſtered ſcene: a rich and beautiful Baſon, hemmed in on every ſide; the valley to the North being cloſed with ſteep winding banks hung with Coppice wood; and, on the other hand, the riſing grounds and woods of Pickſton forman impervious ſkreen; the Exmore Hills juſt ſhowing themſelves above the middle ground of the view; a meek, modeſt, lovely little picture.

Walk upon the Hill above the Town.

A charming view, from the midway of the ſteep, of the valley below (in this point of view alſo cloſed in as a baſon), including Pickſton.

Reach a deſerted place of view, on the ſummit of the hill; and catch a moſt intereſting detail of the winding valley of Dunſbrook; the eye tracing it within the wilds of Exmore: ſteep, narrow, and

thickly

thickly wooded; with a flip or coomb, of water formed land, waving with the ftream; a finely alpine fcene.

At a fharp bend of the valley, immediately under the eye, and facing a long reach, that points to the North Weft, the Coppice wood is cut down, by the wind, in a very fingular manner; even at this diftance---twelve or fifteen miles---from the Sea. But the bleak air of Exmore may, alone, be equal to produce the effect.

The foil of this Eminence is dark-colored and fertile, to its higheft ridge.

Large fatting Wedders now grazing upon it.

Some fine Cows, on a neighbouring fwell.

Whichever way the eye is turned, it meets with fomething rich or beautiful. But perhaps its judgement has been warped by meeting with more than was expected. The ftyle of fcenery is fingular. There is much in the fituation of Dulverton that reminds me of Blair of Athol; though, in fcenery, they fomewhat differ.

DULVERTON

DULVERTON

TO

TIVERTON.

(Thirteen Miles)

THURSDAY, 18 SEPTEMBER, 1794.

PASS under Pickſton Houſe, a low white building, within a deer paddock.

Many ſheep obſervable in the baſon of Dulverton : all thick-carcaſed, and polled.

Obſerve ſeveral wheel carriages,---carts and waggons,---on this road, and in Dulverton: on their way to and from Minehead, and other parts of the Coaſt.

Three-wheeled barrows, drawn by horſes ; uſed in ſetting about manure.

Beginning to ſow wheat.   Shovel out the interfurrows ; as in Weſt Devonſhire.

The valley contracts, and the tall impending trees, with which its ſides are hung,

G 3   appear

appear to clofe it, as below Blair *. But, breaking through this *pafs*, a wide valley, diverfified with bold rotund knolls, is entered.

Lime horfes feen creeping up the fteep fides of the hills.

More good Cows in the valley,

The road good, and the day fine.

The foil of this paffage is redifh ;—the fubfoil rubble, the lower ftratum rock; feldom-failing criteria of fertile land.

Leave the valley, and furmount a rough furze-grown height.

A few large Beeches fcattered over this Diftrict.

Catch a good back view of Exmore, and feem to leave it,

A wide view opens to the South Weft.

Still keep the hills; a well foiled, upland Diftrict.

See the Exe, at fome diftance, winding at the foot of a tall fteep woody bank; a paffage of natural fcenery,---fketched with a broad free pencil.

Defcend

---

* A Seat of the DUKE OF ATHOL, in the Perthfhire Highlands.

Defcend precipitoufly into another fertile and reclufe plot of Country;—the beautiful Environs of Bampton.

BAMPTON—a fmall mean market town; overlooked by an extenfive Limework, whofe ragged excavations and heaps of rubbifh feem to confpire with the town to disfigure this fweetly defigned paffage of Nature. But the face of a Country cannot be disfigured to a better purpofe, than that of contributing to its improvement. Thefe works are faid to have been carried on, time immemorial, for the purpofes of hufbandry.

The ftrata of thefe Quarries lie fteeply fhelving. The Limeftone, in thick feams of large irregular blocks; divided by thin feams of redifh bafe ftone; and by thicker ftrata of brown earth; fome of it foft and light as foot! and foils the fingers as foot or oker; having every appearance of a valuable pigment. The workmen call it " rotten ftone."

The ftone, in general appearance, re-fembles that of Chudleigh; darkly colored, and interfperfed with white veins; but the Bampton ftone has a purplifh caft, and

fparkles

ſparkles with micaceous particles, and is of a looſer texture, than that of Chudleigh.

The rubbiſh of the Quarries is carried out on horſeback; and the ſtone drawn up to the kilns, in three wheeled HORSE BARROWS;—which, an old Laborer tells me, have been uſed, in this Country, beyond memory.

The conſtruction and dimenſions of one of theſe barrows are as follow : The form is that of the common old-faſhioned wheel-barrow of moſt Diſtricts. The ſides nearly upright, ſomewhat ſpreading outward, and projecting behind the body of the barrow; and are there ſhaped into handles; for the purpoſe of moving it, by hand; or adjuſt-ing it readily to the required ſituation. The hind wheels are fitted upon a ſquare axle, which is placed under the hind part of the body of the implement; and which turns round with them, as that of the Highland, and Cumberland cart. The fore wheel has a drag chain adapted to it, to check the motion of the carriage in deſcent. The three are nearly of the ſame ſize and con-ſtruction : namely, each a circle of thick plank.

plank, about two feet diameter, and bound with iron. The width of the body of the barrow is three feet, behind, two feet six inches, before, and four feet long. The depth of the sides, and of the head and tail boards, twelve inches. The headboard leans somewhat forward, over the fore wheel; which is rather smaller than the hind ones, and turns on iron spindles, inserted in the part of the sides which project before the body of the barrow; as in the ordinary wheelbarrow. The draft is by common crane-neck staples, fixed on the outside of the fore part of the implement, near the pivots of the fore wheel *

The fuel of these Limeworks is Welch culm, fetched, by land, from Watchet, sixteen miles.

Draw

* BAMPTON BARROW. This implement might be used with great advantage, on many occasions; especially in moving earth, or other heavy loose materials, a short distance. It is more manageable, by hand, than the Gurry Butt of West Devonshire, and carries a much greater load. I traced it from Dulverton to Tiverton; and saw one near Taunton. I have not observed it, in any other part of the Island,

Draw the kilns, with heartſhaped ſhovels, formed of parallel bars, as the gridiron; the interſpaces ſuffering the aſhes and ſmall lime to drop through; and thus cleaning the ſtone lime, at an eaſy expence of labor. The price of ſtone lime, three ſhillings the hogſhead;—of the aſhes, two ſhillings, for the uſe of the Maſon!

Several orchard grounds, in the neighbourhood of Bampton.

Aſcend a long ſteep hill, and catch another back view of Exmore, and of the finely diverſified environs of Bampton and Dulverton.

Reach a rough, improveable, red-ſoiled height; from which Dartmore, for the firſt time, is ſeen riſing to the view.

The Exe ſtill continues to wind among high upland ſwells, which riſe on either ſide of it: the ſurface gently billowy; the Downs of the Southern Counties, or the Wolds of Yorkſhire, in a ſtate of incloſure.

The Soil, Subſoil, and Road, red.

A dunged fallow: the firſt obſerved, in this journey.

Field

Field ſtacklets common.

Paſs between Beechen coppice-hedges.

The VALE OF EXETER burſts open, with fine effect.   Alſo a broad view of the more Eaſtern confines of Devonſhire preſents itſelf.

Now, a rich Vale view, of the Bradnich quarter of the Vale of Exeter, is ſpread under the eye.

Deſcend, by a long broken ſteep, to TIVERTON.

REMARKS.

The elevation of this paſſage is very great, for a well-ſoiled cultivated Diſtrict. The higher lands are nearly equal in elevation to the Exmore hills; yet

The climature is forwarder than that of the North coaſt, whoſe lands lie lower: the harveſt, here, is entirely finiſhed.

The surface billowy, in the ſtricteſt ſenſe: no regular ridge and valley.   The river and brooks ſeem to wind among the hills.

The

The foil, in general, is rich and productive, as that of Vale Diſtricts; except
the very ſummits of a few of the higheſt
hills.

The ſubſoil, of the beſt lands, is invariably
a flatey rubble; the under ſtratum, a looſe
rock, broken into checkers or long-cube
pieces, of ſizes according to the depth at
which they lie; enlarging in ſize as the
depth encreaſes; until the rock becomes
cloſe and firm.   The *ſubſtance* of this rock,
whether entire or broken, appears to be the
ſame as that of Slate, but wanting its lami-
nated *texture*.

FUR-

FURTHER

GENERAL REMARKS

o n

NORTH DEVONSHIRE *.

THE Inhabitants, throughout, appear to be civilized and intelligent; the lower clafs differing much, in thefe refpects, from thofe of the mining country.

Their fuel—wood and Welch coals.

Their employments—hufbandry, and the worfted manufactory.

The Farmers appear to be of the middle and lower claffes : moftly, plain, decent-looking, working Hufbandmen, of twenty to fifty or a hundred pounds a year. I faw few, if any, which appeared to be of the fuperior order of Farmers.

The woodlands are moftly in a ftate of coppice.—Some timber ; but not much

large

* For former Remarks, fee page 77.

large Ship timber obferved; except between Okehampton and Torrington.

The Orchard grounds of this Diftrict appear to be inconfiderable, compared with thofe of the other Diftricts of Devonfhire.

No Rabbit Warren fell under the eye; indeed the lands, paffed through, are in general too good for that application.

To Apiaries, however, the goodnefs of the lands cannot be an objection; yet I obferved few, if any Bees, in this large tract of country.

The ftate of Hufbandry, from this curfory view of it, appears to be fuperior to that of South Devonfhire; and on a par with that of the kingdom at large. In the management of Liveftock, efpecially Horfes, Cattle, and Swine, North Devonfhire, it is probable, has, for fome length of time, paid more than ordinary attention.

DIS-

DISTRICT THE FIFTH.

THE

VALE OF EXETER.

THE information I obtained, refpecting this highly favored Diftrict, and its Rural Practices, arofe in TRAVELLING repeatedly through its central parts, in different directions; in examining, at different times, the ENVIRONS of EXETER, TIVERTON, and HONITON; and in going over that part of the DRAKE ESTATE, which lies within its limits. The Weftern parts of the Diftrict, the neighbourhood of CREDITON, is the only part which has not engaged more or lefs of my attention.

As the materials, which I occafionally gathered, lie fcattered in my Journals, I will

will here collect them into the Regifter
form; as being beft calculated to give a
comprehenfive idea of this interefting paffage of country, which deferves a more
minute examination, than I have been able
to beftow upon it. However, from what
will here appear, we fhall find it refemble
fo much the other parts of Devonfhire,
which have been more clofely examined,
that a minute detail is the lefs requifite.

A GENERAL

A

GENERAL VIEW

OF

THIS DISTRICT.

I. SITUATION. This natural Diftrict is more accurately defined, than any other Divifion of the WEST OF ENGLAND. It accompanies the Exe and its eftuary, from the fea to the Tiverton hills, juft defcribed, which form its Northern boundary. This boundary is continued, towards the Eaft, by Black Down, to the Heights of Honiton; the South-Eaft quarter being contracted, by a range of barren high lands, between the Otter and the Exe. The Weft fide of the eftuary of the Exe is, in like manner, contracted, by Hall Down, and a continuation of the fame range of Heights, to the North of Exeter; where the Vale fpreads

VOL. II.   H   Weft-

Weftward, to the neighbourhood of Crediton. The Northern extreme of Dartmore, or the unproductive lands in its
vicinity, with the range of hills firft mentioned, define its more Weftern boundary.

II. EXTENT. The irregularity of the
outline, of this Vale Diftrict, renders it
difficult to calculate its contents, with
exactnefs. If I were to rifk a random
eftimate, it would be, that, including its
marginal banks, and fome unproductive
hillocks which rife in its area, it contains
about two hundred fquare miles of furface.

III. ELEVATION. This is by far
the leaft elevated extent of furface, in Devonfhire. It may be termed a Vale Diftrict; efpecially the central and more
Southerly parts of it. It is overlooked by
lands of much greater elevation, on almoft
every fide.

IV. SURFACE. There are two modes
of examining and judging of the furface of
a Country, like that which is now under
notice. Its more prominent features, and
greater

greater variations, are beft obferved from the eminences which overlook it : its fmaller inequalitiès, by travelling acrofs it.

I have had abundant opportunities of examining the Vale of Exeter, in both thefe ways. From Black Down, and other Eminences of the Eaftern Confines,—from the Halldown Hills, on the oppofite fide,— from the Tiverton Hills on the North,— and moft efpecially from an infulated Hillock, fome mile or two to the North of Exeter (from whence almoft every fquare mile of its furface is commanded), I have feen its greater variations; and, by travelling between Honiton and Exeter; Honiton and Nutwell, on the Eaftern banks of the eftuary, below Topfham ; between Nutwell and Exeter, by different roads ; and between Exeter and Bradnich, Collumpton, &c. to Taunton ; I have had opportunities of obferving its minor inequalities.

On the whole, it may be faid of this Diftrict, that although it partakes more of the character of a Vale, than any other part of the County, it is barely entitled to that

dif-

diſtinction.   Between Tiverton and Exeter,
it is beſet with prominences of conſiderable
magnitude, obliterating, in ſome points of
view, the Vale character; and between
Exeter and Collumpton, much billowy ſurface intervenes :   neverthelefs, round Ot-
tery, the Clyſts, and along the Eaſtern
bank of the eſtuary towards Exmouth, and
in the environs of Exeter,—we find much
true Vale country: deep rich ſoil, lying
with a ſurface, ſufficiently elevated, and
ſufficiently varied, to admit of mixed cultivation ;   with a portion of low flat lands,
adapted to the production of herbage only.

V. CLIMATURE.   The frequency of
rain, which renders Weſt Devonſhire un-
comfortable to live in, and, in a wet ſeaſon,
ungenial to Agriculture, is much leſs experienced in the Vale of Exeter.   The
paſſing vapours that are ſufficiently buoyant,
to elude the attractive powers of the more
Weſterly mountains, travel undiſturbed over
this paſſage of depreſſed ſurface ; whoſe
climature appears, by the opportunities I
have had of obſerving it, whether in the

Spring,

Spring, or in the Harveſt months, to be forwarder, than that of any other part of the WEST OF ENGLAND, which has particularly engaged my attention.

The winters of this, as well as of the more Weſtern Diſtricts, are mild, compared with thoſe of the central and Northern parts of the Iſland. In the neighbourhood of Exeter, Graſs may be ſaid to grow freely, through the winter months; at leaſt, in moderate winters.

VI. WATERS. The EXE, and its fine ESTUARY below Topſham, are its chief waters. But two principal branches of the Exe, divaricating Eaſt and Weſt, and a portion of the OTTER, with their numerous branchlets, water the interior of the Vale. At Tiverton, the Exe has barely acquired the River character. And even at Exeter, it ranks low among the Rivers of the Iſland,

VII. SOIL. This varies exceedingly, and ſhows the Diſtrict, it covers, to be formed with fragments of various origin.

H 3   This

This diverfity and intermixture of foils will beft appear, in detail, as they fell under my obfervation.

HONITON TO EXETER. The foil various : much deep ftrong good land. Part brown; part ftrongly tinged with red. The firft red foil obferved, in entering the Weft of England.

ENVIRONS OF EXETER. The foil round the Town is a redifh, deep loam, of an extraordinary quality. To the North of the Town, it varies in productivenefs, with the fubftrata. Where the rock does not rife too near the furface, it is productive to the fummits of the higher fwells. On the South, between Exeter and Topfham, a rifing ground, of fome extent, exhibits arable land of the firft quality : Wheat, Beans, and Flax, luxuriating on fome parts of it; other portions of it, being of a lighter weaker quality. Much of the red foil, in the neighbourhood of Exeter, is of a ftrong, argilaceous, binding quality; and, as fuch, differs effentially from the ordinary filiceous foil of the County.

EXETER

EXETER TO NUTWELL (by Heavytree and Bifhop's Clyft). The foil and fubfoil inclined to red, intermixed with a fmall quantity of gravel; the whole hardening, in fome places, into a fort of pudding ftone; which is ufed for ordinary buildings.

ENVIRONS OF NUTWELL *. The foil various: fome ftrong good red land; much dark, pebbly loam, of a tolerable quality; fome light fandy foil; and other ftill poorer, black, and moorlike. At the feet, and hanging on the fides of the marginal fwells, above Woodbury, a cold weak woodland foil is prevalent.

EXETER TOWARDS TAUNTON. The hills, in general, light turnep and Barley land. In the intervening paffages of Vale, a ftrong red loam is prevalent;—good wheat and bean foil. About Bradnich, a rich valley of grafsland.

ENVIRONS OF TIVERTON. The foil, in general, red, and much of it of a fuperior quality: towards Maiden Down, through

H 4   Hal-

---

* The refidence of the late SIR FRANCIS DRAKE, now of LORD HEATHFIELD.

Halberton, three or four miles from Tiverton, is a paffage of red-foiled rich Vale
country.

VIII. SUBSOIL. It might be thought
fuperfluous to detail the remarks on this
fubject, which I made in different parts of
the Vale : let it therefore fuffice to fay,
that the lands of the Vale of Exeter, as
thofe of other Diftricts, are characterized by
their refpective fubftrata, rather than by
their furface foils : that the ftrong red foils
cover ftrata of clay or loam of the fame
color : that the ftrong brown foils are
likewife incumbent on brick earth, of a
kindred color ; that the rich productive
lands, round Exeter, towards Tiverton, and
in various parts of the area of the Vale,
have a peculiar kind of earthy gravel for
their bafis ; and in fome places, as on the
banks of the Exe, a cleaner gravel is obfervable. On the Weft fide of the Vale,
fome of the higher lands have a fort of
flate rock rifing to the foil. But the prevailing fubfoil of the high grounds, which
rife in the area of the Vale, is a red fand.

And

And in an inftance, between Tiverton and
Maiden Down, a variegated fubftratum is
feen; compofed of thin layers of red and
white loam and fand; refembling what is
obfervable in Glocefterfhire, and under the
red lands of Nottinghamfhire. Thefe cir-
cumftances plainly fhow, that the Vale of
Exeter has been formed from various materials, and of courfe exhibits a variety of
lands.

General Remark.

This intermixture of lands is feen, in an
interefting point of view, from the infulated hillock, already mentioned, in the
neighbourhood of Exeter (Stoke Hill I
think it is called).

The deep rich Vale lands are thickly fet
with Hedgerow Elms, pruned up to poles,
and rifing in clofe order, as we fee them in
the Vales of Glocefterfhire, and on the
rich deep lands in the neighbourhood of
the Metropolis ! Has this fpecies of produce, and this peculiarity of practice, rifen
fpon-

fpontaneoufly out of the nature of the
lands? or has the tree, and the method of
treating it, been imported from the Con-
tinent, eftablifhed on the banks of the
Thames, and from thence tranfplanted to
thofe of the Severn and the Exe?

IX. On the POLITICAL DIVISIONS
of this Diftrict, I find few remarks; except
what relates to the fizes of TOWNSHIPS;—
which appear to be fmaller, than what I
have obferved in the other parts of Devonfhire: a circumftantial evidence, this,
among others that will prefently be adduced,
that the fertile Vale under notice was early
cultivated, and thereby acquired an early
population.

X. PUBLIC WORKS. The only IN-
LAND NAVIGATION, which this Diftrict
at prefent enjoys, is that of the Eftuary of
the Exe, to Topfham; with an artificial
Navigation, from thence to Exeter. And,
perhaps, the only CANAL that could be
profecuted with profit, to the County at
large, would be one from Exeter, by Crediton,

diton, to Okehampton, there to join the one proposed, between Biddeford and Plymouth *. And even this I suggest with diffidence, from my not having sufficiently traced the ground, in detail. The *Line* is, in every respect, what could be wished. If this triple Canal should be executed, Devonshire might, with good reason on her side, boast of her acquired, as well as of her natural advantages. Possessed of such a public work, she would stand unrivalled in facility of internal transfer: there would scarcely be a farm in the County, situated at more than one day's journey of a team from water carriage ;—an accommodation, whether in bringing in manures, or carrying off produce, which no other County, I believe, can claim ; and which, in a Country where wheel carriages are, in some cases, difficult to use, would be an advantage to the LANDED INTEREST, scarcely to be calculated.

The ROADS of the Vale are most remarkable for their closeness ; narrow lanes, beset with mounds, and overhung with trees.

* See Page 39.

trees. This charge, however, does not lie, invariably. The more public Roads are, in general, well formed and well kept: the barrel gently convex, and the materials (moſtly ſtone—ſome gravel), properly reduced.

The STATE OF INCLOSURE is the ſame, here, as in the other Diſtricts of the County. The appropriated lands are univerſally incloſed: a few rough ſummits of hills, apparently commonable lands, remain open.

This State of Incloſure is probably of long ſtanding; and, from the ſmallneſs of the fields, obſervable in many parts of the Vale; eſpecially round Exeter and on the Eaſtern banks of the Eſtuary, it is reaſonable to ſuppoſe that thoſe parts, at leaſt, were early incloſed. What ſerves to corroborate this idea, the mounds of the hedges are lower here, than in the Ham Diſtricts; and are, in general, furniſhed with Timber Trees.

XI. The PRESENT PRODUCTIONS of the Lands of the Vale are chiefly ARABLE CROPS and HERBAGE; with a

profuſion

profufion of HEDGEWOODS; and fome ORCHARD GROUNDS; but with very little WOODLAND, in the area of the Vale; not even in the more hilly parts of it.

Neverthelefs, the Diftrict, I underftand, does not fupply itfelf fully with grain; at leaft, not with WHEAT; which is imported, occafionally; and chiefly, I believe, from the Ifle of Wight. But the Country is populous. The Serge Manufactory employs many hands throughout the Diftrict, and finally concenters at Exeter. Yet, of DAIRY PRODUCE, the Vale is enabled to fend fome fupply to the Metropolis.

XII. Of the prefent STATE OF SOCIETY, in this Diftrict, I am prepared to fay but little.

The TOWNS, in general, are populous, cheerful, refpectably built, and finely fituated. The fituation of Tiverton is fingularly fine.

The COUNTRY HABITATIONS are generally mean in their appearance, from the nature of the materials of which they are almoft univerfally conftructed; namely,

red

red earth and thatch. The neatnefs of the
latter, however, is fuch as to render this
fpecies of covering more tolerable and lefs
improvident, here, than it is in countries
where ftraw is beaten to pieces with the
flail, and laid on with lefs dexterity, than
is the " reed" of the Weft of England.
Earthen walls, rough caft, and covered
with a reed roof, form a neat and comfortable habitation.

The EMPLOYMENTS of the Inhabitants
are thofe of *Hufbandry*, and the fame
branch of the *Woolen Manufacture* which
prevails throughout the County : SISTER
EMPLOYMENTS, which ought to pre-
vail, more or lefs, in every Diftrict of the
Ifland.

XIII.   Of the FACE of this fair
COUNTRY it were impoffible to fay too
many fine things.   But, as its goodly features might lofe much of their force in my
own defcription, I will briefly fet it down
at what its *happy* Inhabitants believe and
affert it to be—" the richeft fineft Country
in the world."

THE

THE

RURAL ECONOMY

OF

THIS DISTRICT.

MANAGEMENT OF ESTATES.

THE only particulars which ftruck me
forcibly, relative to this fubjeét, are

  I. Laying out Farm Lands.
  II. Farm Buildings.
  III. Hedgerows.

I. DISTRIBUTION OF FARM
LANDS.   There needs not better evidence
of the firft Laying out of Lands, in this
Diftriét, being different from that of South
Devonfhire, than the fmallnefs of Fields,
and the intermixture of Farm Lands, obfervable in the Vale : at leaft in that part

of

of it which I had the beſt opportunity of examining; namely, the Eaſtern banks of the Eſtuary; which, in theſe particulars, might vie with Eaſt Norfolk.

Whether this intermixture of ſmall fields has ariſen from the lands being diſtributed, originally, among ſmall hand-labor huſband-men, or from their having been once in a ſtate of common arable fields, as in other parts of the Kingdom, and have been kept in that intermixed ſtate, by the nature of life-leaſe-hold, is a point which, probably, might now be difficult to aſcertain.

Where theſe lands ſtill remain under life-leaſe-hold, it is difficult to do away the evil; but, where they are free from that tenure, the impropriety of ſuffering them to remain in ſo unprofitable a ſtate, reſts with the Proprietors and Managers of Eſtates.

II. Of the FARM BUILDINGS of the Vale, little is required to be ſaid. They are, in general, without plan, and meanly built: earth and ſtraw being the chief materials. Even the farm yard fences

are

are of "cobb:" in fome inftances raifed ten or more feet high, with folding doors, wide enough to admit laden pack horfes; and with fheds, perhaps, on the infide: thus forming comfortable ftraw yards, at a moderate expence.

The favorite material of thefe walls appears to be the ftrong red loam mixed with gravel, which has been mentioned, and which acquires, in drying, a ftonelike hardnefs. "If kept dry, it will ftand for ever."

This material of building (earth of various forts under the general name of cobb) has been ufed, here, time immemorial. Barns and dwellii g houfes, of almoft every fize, are built with it. The walls from fourteen inch to two feet thick; the flues of chimneys being carried up with the gables, as in building with ftones or bricks.

III. HEDGEROWS. In this refpect, too, the inclofures of the rich deep lands of the Vale refemble the wood-bound Pightles of Eaft Norfolk.

The Elms of the Hedges have been already noticed. Oak Pollards, and, in some parts, Oak Timber Trees, stand thick on the Hedge banks, or grow out of their sides, or at their bases; with Coppice wood rising between them, as in Kent, and other Districts.

I mention this circumstance the rather, as it forms one of the few distinctions, which mark this Eastern District, from North and South Devonshire *.

WOODLANDS.

ON this subject, nothing of importance struck me, except what relates to the MANAGEMENT of HEDGEWOODS.

The Coppice wood is treated, as in West Devonshire; the Oak stubwood being peeled on the stem.

And

* It is in a manner needless to remark, that the GATE-WAYS of Devonshire are adapted to Horse-and-Crooks, rather than to Wheel Carriages. Even where the latter are in partial use, seven or eight feet is the usual width. GATE POSTS, within the reach of Dartmore, are commonly of Moorstone.

And in the Management of HEDGEROW TIMBER, the only particular, which is noticeable, is that of lopping, not only Elms, but Oaks, to bare ftems! a practice which is not common to Hedgerows, only; but which I have feen extended, in this Diftrict, for the firft time, to Grove Timber! Oak Woods!!

A practice fo deftructive of private property, and public benefit, can only have arifen in a fcarcity of fuel, or in the rapine of tenants, and the neglect of thofe who fhould reftrain them.   Indeed, I would hope that the practice is not univerfal; at leaft with refpect to Wood Timber; but is confined to the eftate which I more particularly examined,

The practice of pruning off the fide boughs of Hedgerow Elms is a venial crime; provided it be not deferred too long from the laft cutting. In the more valuable applications of the Elm, knottinefs of texture is a defirable quality. But in moft, or all, the ufes to which the Oak is applied, a cleannefs of grain is its beft recommendation.

I 2   AGRICULTURE.

AGRICULTURE.

I. FARMS. From the fize of Farmeries, and the appearance of FARMERS, this Diftrict refembles the reft of the County, in the SIZE of its Farms.

II. BEASTS OF LABOR. In this refpect, too, the Vale of Exeter is truly Danmonian. OXEN are ufed in plowing; PACK HORSES in carriages of every kind; even to the gates, and within the ftreets of Exeter. I have feen, in its immediate environs, dung fetting about with "horfe and potts *." In this inftance, three horfes, with a man to fill and two boys to drive, formed the fett. The diftance fifty to a hundred yards. The difpatch far from inconfiderable.

III. IMPLEMENTS.

* See Vol. I. P. 122.

III. IMPLEMENTS. Still we find ourſelves within the limits of Danmonia. The PLOW, here, is more truly heraldic, even than in Weſt Devonſhire. The body longer, and the beam ſhorter : the end of the beam merely ſhooting before the point of the ſhare !

IV. PLAN OF MANAGEMENT. In the ARABLE CROPS of the Vale, we find a deviation from thoſe of the more Weſtern Diſtricts :—ariſing, no doubt, from an alteration in the quality of the ſoil. On the ſtrong cold lands, in the area of the Vale, *Beans* are a common crop ; and, on the richer deeper ſoil, *Flax* is not unuſually grown. And, perhaps, in this part of the County, a greater proportion of Cows are kept for the BUTTER DAIRY. But, in other reſpects, I have detected no obvious marks, in the outlines of Management, which diſtinguiſh this from the more Weſtern Diſtricts of Devonſhire.

V. MANURE. The ſame roof ſhaped heaps of LIME COMPOST, that are common

in South Devonſhire, are obſervable in the
Vale of Exeter. The upper parts of the
Vale are ſupplied with Lime, from the
borders of Somerſetſhire : the central and
Southern parts are ſupplied, by water, with
ſtones, which are burnt at Exeter, and on
the banks of the Eſtuary, after the manner
of Weſt Devonſhire.

I have ſeen no traces of the SHEEP FOLD,
in this or any other part of the County.

VI. WHEAT is here grown on narrow
ridges, generally running diagonally acroſs
the ſlope, as in Weſt Devonſhire, &c.

VII. All the BEAN CROPS, that I
obſerved, were raiſed in the random or
broad caſt manner.

VIII. TURNEPS. The HOING of
Turneps is coming into practice, in the
Vale. I obſerved, in different parts of it,
clean good crops.

IX. GRASSLAND. On the Management of Graſsland, nothing ſtriking, or
remarkable,

remarkable, occurred to me, in this Diſtrict; except an inſtance or two of ſmall parcels, which lie in a rough, unproductive ſtate; apparently for want of being properly freed from ſuperfluous moiſture.

X. ORCHARDS. Many ſmall Garden Orchards are ſcattered, in every part of the Vale. In the Environs of Tiverton, I obſerved ſome full ſized Orchard Grounds. And the Villages round Exeter are en-wooded, with Apple Trees; which are ſtill Danmonian: but, as the borders of Somer-ſetſhire are approached, the ſtems increaſe in length; as will be more particularly noticed, in the VALE OF TAUNTON.

XI. CATTLE. This being a Dairy, rather than a Breeding Diſtrict, a mixture of breeds may be expected. Neverthelefs, in the more remote parts of the Vale, I have obſerved different inſtances of fine Cattle, of the pure North Devonſhire ſort.

In the neighbourhood of Exeter, many Alderney, or "French Cows" are ſeen;

I 4   and

and a mongrel fort, betwen that and the Devonfhire breed, are not uncommon.

XII. The DAIRY. The produce of the Dairy, here, as in Weft Devonfhire, is BUTTER and SKIM MILK CHEESE.

This fpecies of Farm Produce has increafed, of late years ; the butter, even of this extreme part of the Ifland, being now fent, in greater or lefs quantity, to the London Market.

Neverthelefs, the CLOUTING OF CREAM, I underftand, ftill remains the prevalent practice of the Vale ; in which, however, fome "RAW-CREAM DAIRIES" are already eftablifhed : and, as the practice of raifing cream, or fuffering it to rife, in the natural way, has gained poffeffion of the DAIRY DISTRICT (which will prefently be defcribed), on the Eaftern banks of the Vale, there will be little rifque in predicting, that it will require no great length of time, to extend itfelf over the area. How long it will afterwards take it, to climb over the Weftern banks, into South Devonfhire, is much more difficult to forefee.

XIII. What

XIII. What SWINE I have obferved, in the Vale, are of the fame tall white fort, which appears to be common to the County.

XIV. SHEEP. The Sheep which are REARED in the Vale, are chiefly, I believe, of the HOUSE-LAMB BREED.

But the more ordinary ftock of the fmaller Farmers are bred on the Heights about Tiverton; and are the fame varioufly headed race, which is common to all the high lands of Devonfhire and Cornwall.

On the rich grazing lands, below Exeter, I have remarked a large polled breed fimilar to that which has been noticed, about Totnefs. So commonly do Soils invite congenial Stock.

DISTRICT

DISTRICT THE SIXTH.

THE

DAIRY DISTRICT

O F

WEST DORSETSHIRE,

&c. &c,

INTRODUCTORY REMARKS.

THE paſſage of country, to which I have given this appellative diſtinction, is at once NATURAL and AGRICULTU-RAL. Natural, as poſſeſſing a peculiarity, as well as a uniformity of ſtyle, in the formation of its ſurface ;—agricultural, as having the ſame leading object, in its plan of Rural Management.

Neverthelefs, I was led to an examination of it, by circumſtances more fortuitous, than thoſe which attended the ſurveys of ſome

of

of the other Diſtricts, noticed in theſe Volumes.

In my firſt journey, into the WEST OF ENGLAND, being ſtruck with the appearance of the country, about Bridport, I ſtopt a few days to examine it; and went over it, ſome miles round, on either ſide: thus gaining a competent knowledge of the Eaſtern part of the Diſtrict, and a general idea of its Rural practices. In paſſing, repeatedly, between Bridport and Honiton, 1 have had opportunities of ſeeing ſomething of the Center of the Diſtrict. And, in travelling between Crewkern and Chard, and afterwards taking a deliberate view of the Drake Eſtate, lying in the Valley of Yarcombe, I compaſſed the Northern margin, and ſaw much of its Weſtern extremity: thus gaining a comprehenſive idea of the whole Diſtrict; except its South-Weſtern quarter.

But, notwithſtanding the information I had collected, reſpecting the paſſage of country here brought forward, I might, in forming this public Regiſter, have paſſed it, as an intermediate Diſtrict, had it not

con-

conſtituted a ſtriking part of that extraordinary tract, of which theſe Volumes have
hitherto been treating, and of which I am
deſirous to render my account as full as
poſſible.

In attempting to give a comprehenſive
view of this Diviſion of the Weſt of England, I will briefly digeſt the particulars that
ſtruck me, in the curſory views which I
have had of it ; and firſt of the

DISTRICT.

I. SITUATION.   Its boundaries are
the lower flatter Vale lands of Dorſetſhire,
and Somerſetſhire, on the North *.   The
Vale of Exeter, on the Weſt.   The Chalk
Hills

* The indeterminate boundary, on the Somerſetſhire
ſide, may be caught from the following remarks, made
between Crewkern and Chard.

CREWKERN to CHARD.
Leave the Limeſtone lands, at Crewkern.
Aſcend, by a ſandy hollow way, a furze grown Com-
mon, with a gravelly ſubſoil.

Aſcend

Hills of Dorſetſhire, on the Eaſt. And the Sea, on the South.

II. The EXTENT is about twenty miles from Eaſt to Weſt; and twelve or fifteen, from North to South.

III. Its ELEVATION is great. It riſes abruptly from the Sea, by ſteep cliffs, in ſome parts of great height; the loweſt of the ſwells are high upland: riſing, towards the Northern margin, to mountain heights.

IV. SUR-

Aſcend ſtill higher, a chalky hill: a fragment of the Dorſetſhire Downs.

On the left, a Devonſhire Hollow, or " Trough," of fine graſsland.

Extenſive views over Somerſetſhire, towards Taunton.

Paſs Hinton, Lord Poulett's.

Travel on a high ridge of hill (White Down); very extenſive views, into Devonſhire, and Somerſetſhire.

A charming green baſon, at the foot of the hill: large graſs incloſure; with a few hedgerow Elms.

A wide range of Danmonian ſurface; hills and hollows, on a large ſcale, and ſpreading, without limits, towards Devonſhire.

The firſt Devonſhire hedgebank.

Deſcend towards Chard.

IV. SURFACE. By the formation of its surface, this District is most strongly marked; exhibiting the Danmonian style, in all its purity.

Immediately upon the coast, the hills are many of them rotund, and fertile to their summits; but, farther from the Sea, they are mostly flattened on the top, and comparatively infertile with the wide winding vallies, which seem to worm their way in among them; displaying the most broken and *troubled* surface. Still farther towards the Northern margin, especially towards the Western extreme, the ground breaks into more regular ridges and vallies; branching out, in the ordinary manner of mountain surfaces.

The wider Vallies, that have fallen under my notice, are the Valley or Bason of Beaminster; the Valley, or, as it is called, the Vale, of Marshwood; the Valley of Yarcombe *, and that of Upottery: each of

them,

* The VALLEY OF YARCOMBE. This Valley contains part of three Parishes, lying, I believe, in three Counties:

them, except the laſt, containing ſeveral hundred acres of valuable land.

V. CLIMATURE. In the lower lands of this Diſtrict, even in its more Northern vallies, the ſeaſons are early. In 1791, Haymaking was at its height, in the neigh-bourhood of Bridport and Beaminſter, the beginning of July; and, in 1794, Raygraſs was ready to ſhoot into head, in the Valley of Yarcombe, the firſt of May. I ſhould conceive it to be, on a par of years, ten days or a fortnight before Weſt Devonſhire.

VI. WATERS. Each Branch Valley of the Northern margin has its rivulet or brook; which, collecting, form the upper branch of the Otter, the Axe, and the Brook or River of Bridport: the Axe re-ceiving the principal part of the waters of the Diſtrict.

VII. SOILS,

Counties: namely, Membury, in Dorſetſhire; Whit-ſtunton, in Somerſetſhire: and Yarcombe, in Devonſhire: —the laſt comprizing the principal part of its lands.

VII. SOILS. Thefe vary, in different parts of the Diſtrict. In the Bridport quarter,—the lower lands are moſtly of a ſuperior quality—deep rich loams—throwing out full crops of Wheat, Beans, Flax, and Hemp; and, in this part of the Diſtrict, the ſides and even the ſummits of the ſwells and hillocks are many of them well ſoiled; the beſt a limeſtone loam; others of a lighter ſandy nature.

But, in the Valley of Yarcombe, and apparently in the neighbouring Vallies, much of the ſoil is a ſtrong red loam, lying on a cool baſis,—Wheat, Beans, and Oak, land.

The ſoil of the higher hills, throughout this Diſtrict, is a ſandy loam, intermixed with a ſingular ſpecies of ſtone, a baſe kind of flint; a ſpecies of ſoil and accompaniment, which are common to the higher leſs fertile hills of Eaſt Devonſhire, and are extended to the Halldown Heights, on the Weſt ſide of the Vale of Exeter; and which, the flints at leaſt, are peculiar perhaps to this part of the Iſland: I have not obſerved them in any other.

Vol. II.   K   VIII. SUB-

VIII. SUBSOILS. Thefe are various, as the foils, the paffage of country under notice refembling the Vale of Exeter, in this refpect. The cool red foils have a ftrong clayey loam for their bafe ; the rich lands in the environs of Bridport, have either a lighter loam, or a fort of flinty gravel, beneath them : the hills are of fand, intermixed with flints, with here and there a mafs of limeftone.

IX. FOSSILS. The moft ufeful Foffil production, that fell under my notice in this Diftrict, is LIMESTONE ; which is raifed, not in the neighbourhood of Bridport only, but more or lefs in other parts of it. Befide being burnt into Lime, it is ufed as a walling material, as well as for paving Slabs, Drain Bridges, and Stiles ; large Slabs of it being not unfrequently fet onedge for this purpofe. It is alfo ufed as a road material. It appears as a mafs of conglutinated fhells ; refembling much, in general appearance, the Suffex marble : a fpecies of Limeftone dug out of the ftrong

lands

lands of the Wild of Suffex; whereas, this is found on the dry fummits of hills.

On fome of the Northern Heights, detached maffes of CHALK are found;—fragments, probably, of the neighbouring hills. White Down, between Chard and Crewkerne, appears to be chiefly compofed of Chalk; and is the moft Weftern collection of that Foffil, which I have obferved; or which, probably, is found, in this Ifland.

X. ROADS. The Roads, in the more reclufe Vallies, are nearly in a ftate of Nature: the antient Horfe paths of the Foreft ftate: crooked, narrow, numerous, and full of floughs.

XI. STATE OF INCLOSURE. The lower grounds are wholly inclofed; the hills, at prefent, are open; but they fhow evident marks of their having been, heretofore, in a ftate of inclofure and cultivation! difcovering ftrong lines, which, on the wide Commons of Yarcombe and the neighbouring Parifhes, ftill remain perfectly legible;

gible; and which are not yet obliterated, on the higher more barren fummits, in the neighbourhood of Bridport.

Tradition, in this Eaftern Diftrict, as well as in the Weft of Devonfhire, fpeaks of thefe open neglected lands, as having once been *inhabited*. But this ingenious Hiftorian affigns different reafons, for their being abandoned to the neglect, in which we now find them. On the Weftern fide of the County, we are told, it was owing to a decreafed population. But, on the Eaftern, to a widely differing circumftance. Here, the hills were *firft* inhabited; by reafon of the Vallies being, in the early ftages of fociety in this Country, fo full of Wolves, as to be rendered uninhabitable, by the Human Species. In procefs of time, however, the latter crept down the fides of the hills; clearing off the wood, as they defcended; until at length the Wolves were driven away, or deftroyed; the Vallies taken poffeffion of; and the hills, in confequence, given up, for a more fertile foil, and a more genial climature.

This

This marvellous tale of tradition, whatever may have given rife to it *, feems
altogether unneceffary, to explain the phe-
nomenon under notice; as it may be accounted for in a more fimple and reafonable
way; there being nothing different, in the
prefent appearances of thefe Commons,
from thofe of the Commons of North Devonfhire, that are actually, at this time,
undergoing the very operations, which, in
all human probability, moulded the faces
of thofe of Eaft Devonfhire into their
prefent form; and which, heretofore, left
fimilar veftiges of inclofure and cultivation,
on the furfaces of fome of the commonable
lands of Weft Devonfhire †. The moft
ftriking difference between the appearances
obfervable on the Commons of Yarcombe,
and on thofe of Buckland, is, that the lines

K 3   on

---

* TRADITION, when it reaches not farther than a
few generations, is entitled to every refpect, and is frequently good authority. On perilous events, as of war
or peftilence, it is able to go much farther back, than it
is refpecting the ordinary and quiet operations of Agriculture.

† See Vol. I. P. 32.

on the former are much ftronger ; fome of
the ftill mouldering hedge mounds having
no appearance of being more than a century
old ; fome of them, perhaps, are of more
modern date : indeed, incroachments, of a
fimilar nature, are made at the prefent time.

There can be little doubt, I think, of the
truth of the pofition, that it was once the
prevailing practice of Devonfhire, to CUL-
TIVATE ITS COMMONABLE LANDS, in a
manner fimilar to what we have feen practifed, not only on public Commons, but in
private Inclofures, at this time *.

It is reafonable to fuppofe, that, in early
times, the *Afhes* of the fward or coarfer
covering, were depended on, as manure :
and that, afterwards, *Lime* was ufed, as
an additional ftimulus. And it may be
allowable to conjecture, that, through the
means of thefe two powerful ftimulants,—
without returning any part of the produce,
thus extracted, to the foil, — it at length
became fo much exhaufted, as no longer to
repay the expence of cultivation. What
cor-

* See Vol I. P. 149. Alfo Vol. II. P. 48.

corroborates this idea is, that the only part in which I have obferved the practice continued, to the prefent day, is that in which Lime is moft difficult to procure; and where it may not yet have been obtained in fufficient quantity, to lower the lands to the laft ftage of exhauftion.

Having proceeded thus far, I muft mention, here (though fomewhat out of place), a circumftance relating to the COMMON RIGHTS of Eaft Devonfhire: I fpeak more particularly of the Manor of Yarcombe; whofe Commons belong exclufively to the Lord of the foil, and are ftocked (without ftint) by his own tenants, only. The " lands," as they are emphatically called, of other Freeholders, within the manor, have no right of Commonage! A cuftom of manors which may have eluded my refearches in other parts of the County.

Should it be faid, that this circumftance favors the ftory of the Wolves, for that thefe lands were private property of their refpective Lords, and were thrown up for the ufe of their own tenants only, I will not gainfay it. I have, perhaps, already done more than my duty; and I leave it to the Antiquary, whose bent leads him to topo-graphical enquiries, to determine the point.

Therefore, returning to what more im-mediately relates to the subject matter of this Register, I will finally observe, that, whatever may have been the circumstances which led to the inclosure of the Vallies under notice, they were made from the unreclaimed forest state; without the in-tervention of common fields * or stinted pastures; judging, I mean, from their present appearances; which resemble those of the Inclosures of Kent, Hereford-shire, and other Districts; which have been, undoubtedly, inclosed from a state of unre-claimed woodland. The hedgerows are crooked, and furnished with timber; and the banks raised, in *imitation* of those of Devonshire; but are much lower than the

alta-

---

* It is to be observed, however, that, to the East of Bridport, I saw some faint traces of common arable fields: but in the area or the Western parts of the District, I observed no appearances of that sort.

altogether artificial mounds of the more
Weftern part of the County.

XII. The PRESENT PRODUCTIONS
of the Soils of this Diftrict are WOOD
(chiefly of Hedgerows,----not much detached Woodland), --- ARABLE CROPS,
FRUIT TREES, and GRASS;--the laft being
the moft prevalent produce of the inclofed
lands.   The Hills are overgrown with
DWARF FURZE, HEATH, and COARSE
HERBAGE ; a few of the more barren parts
of them being occupied chiefly by heath.

XIII.   The TOWNS of this Diftrict
are BRIDPORT on the Eaft, AXMINSTER
near the center, HONITON on the Weft,
CREWKERNE and CHARD on the North,
with different Sea Ports on the South.

XIV. VILLAGES.   In this particular,
the Diftrict under view is ftrictly Danmonian :   the Villages, that have fallen
under my eye, are inconfiderable ; the farm
houfes and cottages being happily fcattered
over the areas of the Townfhips : a circumftance

cumſtance more or leſs obſervable, perhaps, in every part of the kingdom, where in-cloſures have been made from a ſtate of Woodland, or of Paſturage : cloſe arrange-ments of houſes, in the form of Villages, being moſt obſervable, in Common-Field Diſtricts *.

XV. HABITATIONS. The BUILD-ING MATERIALS, here, are various. Stones of different ſorts are in uſe ; but earthen walls are, neverthelefs, prevalent ; and, on the whole, the habitations of this Eaſtern Diſtrict are much inferior to thoſe of Weſt Devonſhire ; which far excels the reſt of the County, in this particular.

XVI. The PRESENT APPEARANCE of the Face of this Country may be con-ceived,

---

* The LAYING OUT OF TOWNSHIPS, and their PRESENT STATE OF INCLOSURE, are ſubjects ſo very intereſting to a mind employed in Agricultural Reſearches, that no apology can be wanting for the Remarks that are interſperſed in theſe Volumes, reſpecting them ; as no other Department of the Iſland furniſhes ſo many ſtriking facts, relating to theſe ſubjects, as the WEST or ENGLAND.

ceived, from what has been faid, refpecting its Surface, its Productions, its State of Inclofure, and the Diftribution and Style of its Habitations.

Viewed from fome elevated points, where the barren or infertile fummits of the hills only are feen, it has all the appearance of a Mountain Diftrict.

But, in travelling through it, and ftill more in penetrating its reclufer parts, the moft ftriking tranfitions are produced, and compofitions the moft picturable are caught. It is obfervable, however, that the prevailing characteriftic of the views of this paffage of Country is Beauty, rather than picturefque Effect; differing much, in this refpect, from the wilder fcenery of the Weft of Devonfhire.

In Circles of Views, this paffage of Country abounds. The Summit of the Knoll, the Brink of the Sea Cliff, on the Weft fide of the Harbor of Bridport, is an interefting point; commanding Land and Sea Views of the firft caft. On Beaminfter Down, one of the broadeft and richeft circles of fcenery, this Ifland affords, is

feen

feen with every advantage. In variety, extent, and richnefs, confidered jointly, I know nothing that equals it. To the Eaft, the foft billowy furface of the Chalk Hills of Dorfetfhire, even to their farther extreme. To the Weft, the more rugged mountain fummits of Devonfhire, with Dartmore (I believe) rifing in the fartheft diftance. To the North, the rich Vales of Somerfetfhire, backed by the Quantoc and Mendip Hills, with a portion of the Briftol Channel breaking in between them. To the South, the fingularly broken and beautiful furface, in the Environs of Bridport ; the varied fummits of the hills giving feature and additional effect to the Bay of Bridport ; fpreading its ample furface immediately under the eye ; its Weftern Coaft being finely broken and varied, by ragged promontories, and bold cliffs; and its Eaftern terminated, by the Ifle of Portland ; with mackrel fkiffs playing on the furface of the Bay, and with veffels of burden plowing their way acrofs it.

THE

THE

AGRICULTURE

OF

THIS DISTRICT.

THE leading Object, in viewing it, especially its Western quarter, being that of catching OBVIOUS IMPROVEMENTS, in the MANAGEMENT OF AN ESTATE, rather than to regifter the minutiæ of its AGRICULTURE, I am the lefs prepared to enter into a detail of its practices. I fhall therefore confine my remarks to a few general heads.

I. FARMS. The diftinguifhing character of Farms, in the interior of the Diftrict, is Grafsland. There are many which have very little, if any, arable land; being ftrictly DAIRY FARMS.

In

In SIZE, the Farms of this Eaftern Diftrict are conformable to thofe of the reft of the County; being moftly of the lower clafs. But, here, it is not uncommon for one man to hold two or three diftinct Farms: flocking them with cows, and letting them out to dairymen: a practice however which admits not of commendation; and which will be renoticed.

II. FARMERS. Even in the moft reclufe part of the Diftrict, I met with fome intelligent men. And although the ruft of prejudice may not yet be fufficiently worn away, the late memorable change, in the management of the dairy, fhows demonftrably, that the fpirit of improvement is awake, and augurs much for the benefit of the Country.

III. BEASTS OF LABOR. In the interior of the Diftrict, OXEN are in ufe; but, in the Eaftern quarter CART HORSES prevail.

IV. IMPLEMENTS.

IV. IMPLEMENTS   The only thing
that ftruck me, as excellent or peculiar, in
the conftruction of the Farming Utenfils of
this Diftrict, relates to the YOKE ; whofe
draft iron, or ftaple, is inferted, not perpendicularly, as it ufually is ; but diagonally ;
entering the lower angle of the hind part of
the Yoke, fhooting upward and forward to
the oppofite angle ; where it is keyed, in
the ufual manner.   This prevents the bend
of the bow from bearing too hard againft
the throat of the Ox, and is theoretically
good.   How it operates, in other refpects,
in practice, I had not an opportunity of
obferving.

V. PLAN OF MANAGEMENT. In
the general outline of practice, obfervable
in the more Weftern parts of this Diftrict,
we find little which fpecifically differs from
that of the County at large.   The OBJECTS
are nearly the fame, and the means ufed in
obtaining them fimilar.   The difference
lies chiefly with the proportional quantity
of each fpecies of produce.   In Eaft, as in
Weft Devonfhire, the objects are permanent
grafs,

grafs, arable crops, and temporary leys: part of the grafs, in both Diftricts, being applied to dairy cows, for butter and fkim cheefe. But the proportion of Grafsland, and the proportional number of cows, is much greater here, than in the Weftern parts of the County. Of the lower grounds of the Valley of Yarcombe, four fifths, perhaps, are in a ftate of grafs, permanent or temporary; and this is chiefly depaftured by cows; the number of working cattle being few, and the fheep and young cattle chiefly confined to the hills, and upper grounds.

The ARABLE CROPS of the interior of the Diftrict are chiefiy *Wheat*, and *Oats*; no *Beans!* and but little *Barley*.

The SUCCESSION is fimilar to that of Weft Devonfhire: ley ground, partially fallowed for wheat, with one or two crops of oats; grafs feeds being fown with the laft crop. Some take oats, wheat, oats; agreeably to the practice of the Midland Diftrict; whofe foil and fubfoil are very fimilar.

In

In the more Eaftern parts of the Diftrict, there are fhades of difference obfervable in the Plan of Management: which, probably, partakes more or lefs of that of the Vales of Dorfetfhire, and the rich low lands of Somerfetfhire, from which this part of the Diftrict, now under view, is feparated by a narrow ridge of hill, only.

But what marks the Rural Management of the Environs of Bridport moft evidently, is the culture of *hemp* and *flax*,—to fupply the confumption of a MANUFACTORY of SAIL CLOTH and CORDAGE (from the cable of a man of war, to the fineft packing thread), which has long been carried on, there: giving employment to the female villagers of the neighbourhood; and, of courfe, operating as a mutual benefit to Agriculture and Commerce. A mutual good, however, which can only fubfift, in a rich-foiled Diftrict.

VI. MANURES. LIME is more or lefs in ufe, throughout the Diftrict: being burnt, from ftone found within it, with Welch culm; at leaft in the Bridport quarter.

Formerly, much " MARL" has been ufed, in the valley of Yarcombe ; which exhibits " marl pits" of confiderable capacity, and old enough to have produced Oaks of con- fiderable fize ; perfectly refembling the " marl pits," and the " marl" of the Mid- land Counties : namely, a red clayey loam, without the leaft proportion of calcareous matter in its compofition ! and, what is noticeable, the marl of this Diftrict, as that of the Midland Counties, is now giving way to lime : the change, if one may judge from general appearances, having taken place about the fame period of time !

In the Bridport quarter, I obferved the SHEEPFOLD, in more than one inftance ; agreeably to the Dorfetfhire practice.

VII. GRASSLAND. Notwithftanding this may be confidered as the main object of the Diftrict under view, I obferved nothing praifeworthy in its Management. In the Valley of Yarcombe, where the foil is tenacious, and the fubfoil retentive, the Grafslands, whether permanent or tempo- rary, are injured by fuperfluous moifture :

an

an injury which is not fo much owing to a want of draining, fubterraneoufly, as from their lying too flat, to fhoot off, with proper effect, the fuperficial waters. The natural confequence is, much of the furface is over-run with aquatic weeds and the coarfer graffes, when it ought to be occupied by nutritious and more profitable herbage:

It is to be obferved, that the Spring WATERS of this Diftrict are of an ameliorative quality, and that they are here, as in Weft Devonfhire, partially, and inaccurately, led over the Grafslands.

VIII. ORCHARDS are common, in every part of the Diftrict. I bring them forward, here, merely to fay of them, what may be readily conceived, that, with refpect to the ftature of the trees, and the order in which they are arranged, they form a mean between the Orchards of Devonfhire and thofe of Somerfetfhire. The ftems are, here, fomewhat taller, than in Weft Devonfhire, but are confiderably fhort of the Englifh ftandard. And, in the clofenefs

L 2   of

of arrangement, they ftill more refemble the Devonfhire Orchard. I fpeak more particularly of thofe of the Valley of Yarcomb *.

IX. THE DAIRY   This has been, time immemorial, a Dairy Diftrict. Formerly, its produce was CHEESE, made from the neat milk ; probably of the Somerfet-fhire kind, fold under the name of Bridge-water Cheefe ; fome of which I have met with of a very fuperior quality.   The Valley of Yarcombe was noted for its pro-duce, which was known in the Vale of Exeter, by the name of Membury Cheefe. Indeed, its foil and herbage are fuch, as never fail to produce fine Cheefe, if properly manufactured.   It is naturally a Cheefe Diftrict.

Neverthelefs, of late years, its produce has been changed to BUTTER, for the
London

---

* In approaching thefe Hills, from the Eaftward, the Orchards of Chard were the firft that ftruck me, as par-taking of the Devonfhire Orchatd.   The ftems fhorter than thofe of Dorfetfhire and Somerfetfhire ; but tall enough for young Cattle to pafture beneath the Trees.

London market ; to which it is fent in tubs,
as from the North of England : a change
which has been brought about, by the
powerful influence of the London prices,
compared with thofe of the Country.

The SIZES OF DAIRIES, judging from
what fell under my own obfervation, rife to
thirty or forty Cows. I faw one of near
forty.

The BREED OF COWS, employed in thefe
Dairies, is that of the WEST OF ENGLAND;
namely, the well formed, clean, middle-
horned breed, which is common to the
Counties of Somerfet, Devon, and Cornwall. In the neighbourhood of Bridport,
I faw a tolerably good Dairy of Cows, of a
mixed breed ; apparently a crofs between
the middle and the long horned breeds.

Formerly, the Cows ufed in thefe Dairies
were chiefly REARED, in the Country;
but, of late ears, Butter has borne fo profitable a price, as to induce the Farmers to
forego the rearing, and to PURCHASE their
Cows : a practice which, if it fhould continue, will foon introduce a mixture of
ftock.

L 3   Of

Of the DAIRY MANAGEMENT, of the Diftrict under view, I can fay little: I collected nothing on the minutia of practice worth regiftering. Its prefent practice can fcarcely be faid to be, as yet, *eftablifhed*. It was not, therefore, an object; even had I had leifure to attend to it. To regifter the minutiæ of the Dairy Management, fo as to render the detail intelligible and ufeful, is a tedious and irkfome tafk; and requires, not only time, but a fpecies of opportunity, which did not occur to me, in this Diftrict.

Many of thefe Dairies are LET to DAIRY-MEN, at a certain rent for each Cow; the Farmer keeping up the flock, and fupplying them with pafturage and winter food; and finding a dwelling as well as a dairy houfe, for the renter. It is common for opulent men to hold a plurality of farms, and to let them out to under tenants, in this way: a practice which is injurious to an eftate; as tending to let down the buildings and the fences of farms, thus occupied by under tenants; who have not fo permanent an intereft, in keeping them up, as a leffee, or firft tenant, who makes the place his refidence,

refidence, and expects to occupy the pre-
mifes for a length of time ; and who is
himfelf liable for dilapidations.

X. SHEEP. I obferved, in the Bridport
quarter, fome fine flocks of DORSETSHIRE
EWES : kept as breeding flocks ; fimilar to
thofe of the Vale of Exeter, and Weft
Devonfhire, which have been already
fpoken of. The Sheep of the higher hills
are of the fame mountain fort, which occupy the other hills of Devonfhire and
Cornwall,

SOME

SOME

H I N T S

FOR THE

IMPROVEMENT

OF

THIS DISTRICT.

IT has been mentioned, that my chief
intention, in going over it, efpecially
its Northweftern quarter, was that of en-
deavoring to point out the probable means
of its Improvement   And although my
examinations, and the refult of them, were
moftly of a private nature; fome of the
Remarks, they gave rife to, may, neverthelefs, bear the public eye, and may be
more or lefs ufeful, to thofe who have property in the Diftrict, and who are defirous
to improve its condition.   Nor may the
fuggeftions, here thrown out, be altogether
inapplicable to other Diftricts.

The

The few fubjects of Improvement which I can bring forward, here, with propriety, are,

I. The HILLS, or COMMONABLE LANDS. Something has been already faid refpecting the PRESENT STATE of thefe lands; fo far as relates to their foil, and the marks of cultivation which appear on their furfaces.

The SOILS, however, are various in quality. Some of thefe hills are covered with a loamy foil, of fufficient depth and texture to admit of profitable cultivation *: while others are nearly deftitute of mold. The latter, very fortunately, is by far the fmaller proportion.

The PRESENT PRODUCE has been mentioned, as being furze, heath, and the coarfer graffes: interfperfed, however, with patches of fward.

The

---

* At the head of the Valley of Yarcombe, cultivation and permanent Inclofures climb up the fide—there a gentle flope hanging to the North—and fpread over the top of the hill. And fome of the foil of the Common appears to be of a quality, fimilar to that of the cultivated Inclofures.

The PRESENT STOCK is an inferior kind of Sheep; and young Cattle.

The MEANS OF IMPROVEMENT appear, to me, to be thofe which I have fuggefted, above, for the improvement of DART-MORE *.

The firft ftep is to feparate the culturable from the unculturable lands;—to cut off the fteep ragged brows of the hills, for PLANTING. And the next, to inclofe the flatted tops of the hills, for CULTI-VATION; or for open SHEEP WALK, or RABBIT WARREN; agreeably to the foil and furface, and conformably with the Pro-pofals already offered †.

II. HEDGEROWS. Among the va-rious Improvements of which the LOWER GROUNDS, VALLEY LANDS, or " BOT-TOMS," as they are called, are capable, none ftrikes the eye more forcibly, than that of its HEDGEROW TIMBER; which is, at prefent, in a ftate of neglect. The fame unpardonable practice of lopping Oak
Timber

* See P 29.
† See as above.

Timber Trees, fo fhamefully prevalent in
the Vale of Exeter, is extended, in fome
degree at leaft, to this Diftrict. The foil
of thefe Valley lands is peculiarly fuitable
for the growth of Oak Timber ; and, on
the broad hedge banks, which interfect
them, Ship Timber of the firft quality
might be raifed, in great abundance, with
little injury to the Occupiers of the lands,
compared with the advantages which would
therefrom accrue to the Proprietors and
the Public.   Yet we fee thefe valuable
nurferies, in many parts deftitute, or very
deficient, with refpect to this ineftimable
article of produce : owing, principally or
wholly, to neglect, or a want of fkill, in the
Management of Eftates.   The COPPICE
WOOD of thefe Hedgerows being reaped
by the Tenants, they have an intereft in
deftroying, and preventing the growth, of
TIMBER TREES : a circumftance which
calls for double diligence, on the part of
thofe who have the fuperintendance of
Eftates.   There is, evidently, fufficient
room, in the wide Hedgerows of thefe
lands, to grow an abundance of fuel, for
the

the Tenants, and a valuable supply of Timber, for the Landlord, and the Public.

The means of Improvement are evident. Take down the trees, that are irrecoverably maimed, or which are stunted, or fully grown, and *number* those, which are proper to be left standing. Train up the young stands, or timberlings, so as to give them length of stem ; not more to improve them as Timber Trees, than to prevent their doing unnecessary injury to the crops on either side, and to the Coppice wood, which shall hereafter rise beneath them. And set out, in vacant spaces, at every fall of Coppice wood, such promising shoots, as seldom fail to rise among Coppice wood, growing on a soil so favorable to the Oak, as that of the Valley Lands which are now under consideration.

The last is a business which requires particular circumspection. It cannot, for obvious reasons, be left to a Tenant or his workmen, with safety ; at least not to Tenants in general. The only way, in which it can be done with a certainty of success, is to send round an experienced

and

and faithful Woodman, previoufly to the cutting feafon, to fet out, and diftinguifh with paint, or other confpicuous and permanent mark, the plants which are proper to be left for ftandards.

In this Diftrict,—where the ordinary Woods are ufually cut out, in winter, leaving the Oak ftanding, until the barking feafon, agreeably to the Danmonian practice,—there would feem to be a favorable time for marking the ftandards, between thefe operations. But when it is confidered, that the feedling plants, which ought always to be chofen where a choice offers itfelf, are frequently of inferior fize to the fapling fhoots from the ftubs, and generally too inconfiderable to be left for peeling, fuch interval of time is too late. We may, therefore, without hefitation or hazard, give it in opinion, that every OAKLAND ESTATE, having wide woody Hedgerows, fhould have an eftablifhed regulation, requiring its tenants to give due notice of their intentions, previoufly to the cutting of their Hedgewoods; in order that the proper plants, they contain, may be marked

for

for ſtandards; they being allowed a full
compenſation for the wood thus marked,
as well as for the attention and care which
may be requiſite, in preſerving them from
injury : giving due encouragement to the
tenants, who encourage the growth of
Timber upon their reſpective farms ;—and
treating with neglect, thoſe who are neg-
ligent of its preſervation.

For Remarks on Training Hedgerow
Timber, and its Effects on Arable Crops,
ſee PLANTING and RURAL ORNAMENT,
Vol. I. Pages 56 and 96.

III. PLAN OF FARM MANAGE
MENT. Some alteration, in the arable
department of Management, ſeems to be
wanted. The temporary leys are moſtly
foul, weak, and thin of herbage ; owing,
doubtleſs, to the practice of taking two or
three grain crops, in ſucceſſion, and laying
the land down in a ſtate of exhauſtion, as
well as foul, and out of tilth. Perhaps
taking a crop of beans, in rows well cleaned,
between the wheat and the oat crop, might
be found doubly beneficial ; as introducing
a ſpecies

a fpecies of produce, new to the foil; and ferving to prepare it for the reception of the grafs feeds, by a fallow crop. In cafes where the foil is very foul, a whole year's fallow is, of courfe, requifite.

IV.   In the MANAGEMENT of the SOIL, two or three Improvements are obvious.   Much UNDERDRAINING is wanted; not only in the meadows or lower lands; but on the rifing grounds and hangs of the hills.   Stones are plentiful; and fod drains might be found to anfwer on the ftronger lands.

Another Improvement, which prefents itfelf, in the Management of the Soil, relates to the method of LAYING IT DOWN TO GRASS.

In Weft Devonfhire, where the fubfoil is abforbent, and the foil friable and firm, it is perfectly right to lay it down, as flat and fmooth as poffible.   But, here, where the foil is tenacious, and the fubfoil retentive, and much of it kept in continual furcharge, by the waters pent up beneath it, the practice is in a degree abfurd.   Neverthelefs, the

the practice of thefe two diftant Diftricts, with refpect to the depofiting, or forming the furface of their foils, with the plow, to receive the given crops, is precifely the fame. For wheat, the foil is gathered up into narrow ridges; and is laid flat, for every other crop.

The Improvement which ftrikes me, as proper to be propofed for this Diftrict, is that of keeping the land in ridges, of half a ftatute rod in width, for every crop; or of preferving the prefent narrower ridges for wheat, and throwing two of them together, for beans, oats, and ley herbage : being ever mindful to form the furfaces of the ridges gently convex, to fhoot off the fuperfluous rain water which falls on them ; with deep narrow interfurrows, to receive the water ; and with crofs trenches, to convey it away, to the neighbouring ditches and common fhores : a principle of Management, which is applicable to all cool retentive foils, in the Ifland.

V. MANURES. In a remote fituation, like that which is now more particularly

under

under notice, every experiment and expedient fhould be ufed, to meliorate the condition of its lands, and to make up for the lofs, they annually fuftain, by the produce carried off, without any foreign fupply or return for fuch exhauftion. Lime appears to be the only extraneous, or factitious Manure, at prefent in ufe : a Manure whofe operation is generally weak, on cool, cohefive lands.

In the RURAL ECONOMY of YORKSHIRE, I ventured to fuggeft, as a probable means of meliorating ftrong cohefive foils, the burning of their furfaces;—not more for the afhes, as a Manure, than for the cinders, or BURNT CLAY, which fuch a procefs neceffarily produces, as a means of improving the contexture of fuch cohefive foils * And I have lately been informed, that the burning of the clay of drains, and fpreading it over the ftrong cohefive lands of Somerfetfhire, is now practifed, with great advantage. Thefe fimple and cheap operations are, at leaft, fubjects of experiment, in every Diftrict, whofe lands are of a clofe retentive nature.

VOL. II.   M   The

* See YORK. ECON. Vol. I. Page 313.

The lands, now immediately under confideration, have another probable means of
Improvement within their reach; and
which can rarely be commanded, by lands
of a fimilar nature. I mean the BLACK
MOORY EARTH of the heaths, which inclofe and overlook them. There is doubtlefs much earth of this kind, which lies at
prefent ufelefs on the hills. and which cannot, there, be turned to fo ufeful a purpofe,
as, in much probability, it may, in the
Vallies: applying it, either in a fimply
digefted ftate ;—or in compoft with lime ;
or in the ftate of coal, or of afhes ;—as a
fhort courfe of experiments, attentively conducted, could not fail to determine.

DIS-

DISTRICT THE SEVENTH.

THE

VALE OF TAUNTON,

AND ITS

ENVIRONS:

TOGETHER WITH

CURSORY REMARKS

IN A JOURNEY THROUGH

SOMERSETSHIRE.

IN September 1791, on my way from West Devonshire to Sussex, I stopt some days at TAUNTON ; to look round its fine Environs ; and to get a general view of the Natural Characters, and some insight into the Rural Management, of this celebrated Passage of Country. I, then, not only

examined

examined the Area of the VALE, on either
fide, but afcended the QUANTOC and the
BLACKDOWN HILLS, which over look it;
and went into one of the SEDGEMORES,
which mark Somerfetfhire fo difcriminately,
from the reft of the Ifland.

I have, fince, had repeated occafions to
travel through the Vale: and, in the autumn
of 1794, on leaving Devonfhire, I renewed
my attention; continuing my Remarks
THROUGH THE COUNTY, in the line between Tiverton and the Devizes.

In making out this fketch, I find it moft
convenient to myfelf, and I believe it will
be found moft advantageous to the Reader,
as being moft perfpicuous, to keep thefe
Paffages diftinct: treating of the Vale, as
the main fubject; and joining the reft, as
appendices.

THE

VALE OF TAUNTON.

THE SITUATION of this fertile Vale or Diſtrict, is in the Weſtern Quarter of Somerſetſhire. Its NATURAL BOUNDARIES are, on the North, the Quantoc Hills, which ſeparate it from the Vale of Bridgewater: on the South, the Blackdown Hills, which ſever it, in a ſimilar manner, from the Vale of Exeter:—and, on the Weſt, the Skirts of Exmore and the broken hilly Diſtrict of the Coaſt. On the Eaſt, it is leſs accurately defined;—the riſing grounds of Curry, and the extenſive marſh of South Sedgemore, may be conſidered as its natural boundary.

Its EXTENT is ſmall. It is barely entitled to the diſtinction which is here given it, and which it not uncommonly bears; though, in natural characters, its

dimenſions

dimenfions apart, it is, in the ftrict fenfe, a *Vale Diftrict.* One hundred fquare miles, I apprehend, would contain the whole of its more valuable lands.

The ELEVATION of its Area, above the fea's furface, is, even at prefent, inconfiderable; yet is fufficient to keep it dry and healthy. Nor does any part of it, except its lower extreme, appear to have ever been liable to the tide, or collected floods: it contains none of fuch level marfhes, or "moors," as are fcattered in the central and Southern parts of Somerfetfhire.

In SURFACE, as has been intimated, this Diftrict takes the Vale character. Its area is diverfified with rifing grounds, and interfperfed with low meadowy lands. The banks, on either fide, rife to a great height. On the South fide, the foot of Blackdown fhelves fmoothly, though fomewhat fteeply, into the Vale; but, on the North, the Quantoc Hills rife abruptly, and with a more broken and ftrongly featured front. From Cotherfton Lodge, which crowns a prominent knoll, that juts out from thefe hills, the entire furface of

the

the Vale is commanded. It is clofed, to the Weft, by a crowd of hillocks,—in tumult wild affembled: a genuine paffage of that fingular fpecies of furface, which is common to the Weftern extreme of the Ifland; and which may be faid to terminate, or rather to commence, here.

The CLIMATURE of this Vale might be prejudged, from its fituation. The bafes of high extended hills are generally cool; and backward, with refpect to feafons:—efpecially if they face the North; and ftill more efpecially, if the fubftrata are of a cohefive retentive nature; as are thofe of the South fide of the Vale of Taunton. In the fecond week of September 1791, much barley was ftill unharvefted, and fome uncut.

The SOILS of this, as of many other contracted Vale Diftricts, vary in quality, with the hills which form them. Much of the North fide of the Vale of Taunton is a deep rich fand—a carrot foil: while the oppofite fide is chiefly the fame ftrong red loam, which we have found in the Valley of Yarcombe, and in the Vale of Exeter;

M 4 and

and alfo, in fmall plots, in the South
Hams, and in North Devonfhire.

The SUBSOILS are ftill more various.
In the area of the Vale, a Gravel is feen :
under the rich red fands of Bifhop's Ly-
diard, a concrete fubftance of the fame
color, and of various degrees of hardnefs,
prevails. This concretion, in fome places,
takes the nature of rock; which, on being
expofed to the air, acquires a great degree
of hardnefs, and is ufed as a building material. Under the ftrong red foils, of the
oppofite fide of the Vale, a deep loam, of a
fimilar nature, is found : and, under this,
fubftrata of white fandy fubftance, hardening in fome inftances into a kind of ftone
is feen interlayered with red loam; an
accompaniment, perhaps, which is common
to all the ftrong red lands of the Ifland.

The RIVER of the Vale is the Tonf,
or Taun,—which is rendered NAVI-
GABLE to Taunton. The freightage is
chiefly, Welch Coals, for fuel, and Culm,
for burning Lime.

The chief PRODUCTION of this fertile Diftrict is, at prefent, Corn. There
is

is very little GRASS obfervable; unlefs near the Towns; and by the fides of the Tone, and its branches. And, even from the commanding point of Cotherfton, not more than two or three fmall plots of WOODLAND are feen, in the area of the Vale. The HEDGEROWS, however, are full of wood; and, when viewed from the oppofite banks, a greater degree of woodinefs appears.

The whole is in a STATE OF IN-CLOSURE; with FIELDS of various form and fize.

FENCES. In the Vale of Taunton, we trace, by broken fteps, the decline and termination of the DANMONIAN FENCE.

In the more Weftern and central parts of the area of the Vale, the prevailing Fence refembles that of the Valley of Yarcombe, and the lower grounds of the Vale of Exeter: namely, a low broad bank, loaded with coppice wood, and hedgerow timber trees: the former moftly Oak; the latter Elms, fhorn of their boughs, as in the ordinary practice of the kingdom.

But, in paffing down the Vale, the HAW-

THORN

THORN HEDGE begins, by degrees, to mix with the coppice mounds, and, before the Eaftern extremity is reached, becomes the prevailing Fence.

In the MANAGEMENT OF FARMS, the Vale of Taunton differs, in fome re-fpects, from the DANMONIAN HUS-BANDRY; efpecially in the outline or PLAN OF MANAGEMENT. It is properly an ARABLE DISTRICT: the TEMPORARY LEY, which is common to Devonfhire, fcarcely appears to extend into this Vale In the fecond week of September, half the Diftrict, as feen from the hills, was PLOWED GROUND, or TURNEPS! the reft appeared to be PERMANENT GRASS, with the CORN, then unharvefted, and STUBBLES unbroken up.

Neverthelefs, in MINUTIAL PRACTI-CES, particularly in the management of Lime, the burning of Beat, and the fowing of Wheat, the Vale purfues the Devonfhire method.

The CROPS are *Wheat, Barley, Oats,* and *Beans,* the laft more efpecially, on the ftronger lands of the South fide of the Vale.

ORCHARDS.

ORCHARDS. The height of Orchard trees, as of Hedges, undergoes a change in this Diſtrict. In travelling, between Exeter and Taunton, the ſtem of the Apple tree is ſeen to lengthen towards Somerſetſhire, but not in uniform progreſſion. And, in paſſing from Tiverton, into the Vale ſimilar appearances are ſeen. The firſt full-ſtemmed *Engliſh* Orchard was obſerved, in the neighbourhood of Wellington.

But as this and other particulars, relating to the remarkable tranſition,—obſervable in Rural Practices, on leaving the Weſtern Peninſula, or extreme part of the Iſland,—will appear in the following JOURNAL, it is unneceſſary to enter farther, in this place, on the particular management of the Vale of Taunton.

THE

THE

QUANTOC HILLS.

THESE form a narrow range of Mountain Heights, which rife near the junction of the Parret and the Tone, below Taunton, and lead, in a Northweft direction, towards the Coaft of the Irifh fea, or Briftol Channel; dividing the low fertile lands of the Vale of Taunton, from thofe of the Vale of Bridgewater.

Their ELEVATION, with refpect to the adjoining lands, is confiderable; though their pofitive height, above the tide, is not great. They are, however, too high, and too mountainlike, in their general afpect, to be merely deemed upland; yet not of fufficient importance to be ftyled mountain.

The SURFACE of thefe hills, or rather chain of hills, is greatly diverfified. They refemble, in furface, foil, and prefent produce, the hills of Eaft Devonfhire; and, like thofe, have been heretofore cultivated (in whole or in part) : the vallies or breaks,

between

between them, being now in a ſtate of cultivation.

The soil of the extended ſummit, to the
Eaſt of Cotherſton Lodge, appears to be of
a nature that would pay for cultivation,
being now chiefly covered with graſs and
the upland ſedges.   But, to the Weſtward
the ſoil appears to be more barren, and
much of the produce heath.

There being evident traces of Limeſtone
on theſe hills, their IMPROVEMENT, in
much probability, might be rendered very
profitable, to individuals.

The inſulate ſituation of theſe Hills renders them highly intereſting, to thoſe who
admire the ample ſcenery of Nature. The
Mendip Hills and the principal part of
Somerſetſhire which lies to the South of
them; the Hills of Wiltſhire and Dorſet
ſhire ; Beaminſter Down, with the other
prominent Hills of Eaſt Devonſhire, terminating with Black Down ; diſtant Hills,
in Devonſhire ; Exmore, and the Hillocks
of the Coaſt ; with the Briſtol Channel and
its Holms, backed by the Welch Mountains ; ſpread out wide to the view.

THE

THE

BLACK-DOWN HILLS.

IT has been faid, that thefe Hills form the Southern bank of the Vale of Taunton, and feparate it from the Vale of Exeter : and, in like manner, they divide the Counties of Somerfet and Devon. They are a continuation of the Axminfter Hills; forming their Northweftern extremity.

In ELEVATION, they exceed everything in their neighbourhood, equally overtopping the Quantoc and the Axminfter Hills.

In furface, they refemble the reft of the mountain heights of this extreme of the Ifland; namely flat, or fwelling; divided by wide open Dells, or fhallower Dips; and partially fevered, by deep rich Vallies or "Troughs"—as they are called—of cultivated lands. The extreme point, to the Weft, forms a bold Promontory; wearing,

on

on its Northweſtern brow, a mountain appearance.

The SOIL of the ſummit is of an inferior quality; of a black moory nature: and ſtrewed with the ſame baſe kind of *Flints,* that are obſervable on the other hills of Eaſt Devonſhire; and this without any traces of *Chalk:* an unuſual circumſtance worthy of the Naturaliſt's attention.

The STOCK of theſe mountain heights are young cattle of the Weſt of England breed, and moſt of them neat: with the ſame aukward, half-horned breed of Sheep, that are common to all the wild lands of this extremity of the Iſland.

On the Northern hang,—about the mid-way,—of theſe hills, are quarries of LIME-STONE, found in a ſingular ſtate.

The quality of the Stone is evidently that of the Clayſtone of Gloceſterſhire, of Lei-ceſterſhire, and of the Vale of Belvoir; but inſtead of being depoſited in regular ſtrata, it is found in detached fragments, bedded, promiſcuouſly, in pale-colored earth; ſimilar to that with which it is interlayered, in the inſtances above men-tioned;

tioned ;—as if the ſtrata of Stone had been broken to pieces, while the earthy matter was in a plaſtic ſtate, and the maſs had been blended, by ſome violent agitation.

The color of the Stone is blue, internally, and white, towards the ſurface; and burns to a ſomewhat ſulphur-colored Lime; reſembling that of Barrow, in Leiceſter-ſhire *

FURTHER REMARKS ON THE LIME-STONE OF WEST SOMERSETSHIRE.

I afterwards examined the Limeworks and quarries of the Hills, which bound the Vale of Taunton to the Eaſt, and which are entirely detached from the Blackdown and Axminſter Hills.

Here, the ſame Stone is found, in regular unbroken ſtrata; as they appear in the quarries of Gloceſterſhire, Leiceſterſhire, &c. but with a very ſtriking difference reſpecting their ſituation. In the places abovementioned, they are lodged beneath the ſurface of low flat Vale lands; whereas,

in

* See Mid. Econ. Vol. I. P. 28.

in the inftance under notice, they break out of the face of, a lofty and fteep hill.

Neverthelefs, fuch is the impervious and retentive quality of thefe ftrata, that the land which lies over them, even in this elevated fituation, and clofe upon the brink of a precipice, which probably has heretofore been the waterworn cliff of an eftuary or arm of the fea, is cold and ungenial, as that which covers their watery bed, in the low grounds of the Vale of Glocefter. The furface, in many places, is occupied by Coltsfoot. A field, clofe upon the brink of the cliff which overlooks the marfh, or Sedgemore, that will prefently be noticed, was under fallow for Wheat, at the time I was upon thefe Hills (in Sept. 1791); and, from the *complection* of the foil, it appeared to be barely worth the labor of cultivation.

How much more depends on the quality of the fubftratum, than on that of the foil itfelf: the very foil, here under notice, if incumbent on an abforbent fubfoil, would be worth three or four times its prefent value.

Vol. II.   N   SOUTH

SOUTH SEDGEMORE.

FROM the eminence juft mentioned, I had a favorable opportunity of gaining a general view of this rich Level of marfh-lands. And, by riding a few miles within its area, paffing through its herds and flocks, and converfing with thofe who were attending to them,—I had a fimilar oppor-tunity of obtaining the particulars of in-formation, which a curfory view required.

The natural boundaries of thefe marfhes are the Limeftone Heights, abovemen-tioned, on the South and South-Eaft ; on the Weft, the broken bafe of the Eaftern extremity of the Quantoc Hills, and the narrowed *mouth* of the Vale of·Taunton. On the North, the Parret and the Tone are confidered as the boundary of the " Moor" immediately under confideration ; their junction forming the extreme point to the North. But lands of a fimilar

nature

nature are feen to ftretch away beyond that point, to the North-Weft.

In the view from the hills, there appears to be an EXTENT of thefe lands ten or twelve miles in length, and fome miles in width, under the eye. But the outline is extremely irregular.

The ELEVATION of thefe lands (the part I examined at leaft) is fuch as to fecure them, at prefent, from the tide; nor did I learn that land floods incommode them, in any confiderable degree.

Their SURFACE is level as that of the water, which, with moral certainty, once occupied the fpace they now fill. If we calculate on the rapid increafe of earthy matter, at the mouths of rivers, whofe waters are collected from rich arable lands; —and on the decreafing depth of the Sea; which, though perhaps not equal to what fome modern Writers conjecture, has probably been confiderable, during the laft millennium of time;—it is reafonable to fuppofe, that fince the firft fettlement of this Ifland, the Sea rolled its rapid tides within

N 2 the

the area now under contemplation: and the rapidity of the tides, in the eſtuary of the Parret, as of the Severn, accounts more fully for the rapid increaſe of land; occaſioned by the ſilt forced up, by the " Boar" or Eagre, which is common to the rivers of the Severn Sea *.

The preſent name of the marſhes of Somerſetſhire, is a ſufficient evidence, to prove, that, at the time it was aſſigned them, the reclaim was not compleated: that they were, at the time it was applied,

in

---

* This ſtriking natural effect, I have repeatedly obſerved, on the banks of the Severn, near Gloceſter; where, at certain times of the tide, and moſt eſpecially during a ſtrong Weſterly wind, a body of water, ſome few feet in depth, ruſhes impetuouſly up the Channel of the river; gliding, as it were, upon the deſcending waters; ruſhing out at the more abrupt bends, and daſhing its ſpray to a very great height, on every obſtruction; attended by ſounds, which may ſometimes be heard to a conſiderable diſtance.

This effect is probably cauſed, by the form and ſituation of the Briſtol Channel; which receives the tide, from the Atlantic, by a wide opening, and contracts towards the mouths of the rivers that are thus affected.

The narrowing eſtuary of the Humber, produces a ſimilar effect.

in a ftate of *Fen*; not in that of firm, dry
Marfhlands, as we now find them.

The SOIL of this marfh is a red loam, of
confiderable ftrength and tenacity; refembling, with great exactnefs, that of the
Ifle of Alney, and the other marfh or
meadow lands of the Severn *; except in
the deeper tinge of red which the foil of
South Sedgemore has received, from a
greater mixture of colored water, which
the red foils of the Vale of Taunton, and
the North Eaftern bafe of the Blackdown
hills, have furnifhed.

The HERBAGE is fingularly fine : apparently the Dogstail (*Cynofurus Criftatus*),
Raygrafs, and White Clover; with, however, fome plots of thiftles, on the drier
parts, and ftripes of filver weed (*Potentilla
Anferina*) on the fides of the drains, and
more fwampy places.

Hence, this extent of marfhes may be
confidered as land of the firft quality : fit
for every purpofe of permanent grafsland.

N 3   The

---

* For farther Remarks on the formation of Marfh and
Meadow lands, fee the RURAL ECONOMY of GLO-
CESTERSHIRE, Vol. I. P. 170.

The STOCK which it bore, at the time I was over it, were Horſes, Cattle, Sheep, and Geeſe.

Of the *Horſes*, I ſaw nothing which ſtruck me as requiring notice.

The *Cattle* conſiſted chiefly of young growing ſtock—moſtly two or three years old. With, however, many Cows; ſome of them apparently in milk, or recently thrown up. The condition of moſt of theſe Cattle was good; many of them were full of fleſh; though the graſs was ſhort, as that of Sheep and Geeſe Commons uſually is round. Aged Cattle, I underſtood, are brought forward on theſe commonable lands, to be finiſhed with afterʼgraſs.

The *Sheep* were chiefly or wholly of the horned breed; and had been put upon theſe lands, for the purpoſe of fatting. In a favorable year, it ſeems, they get tolerably fat. But much drought bakes thoſe clayey lands, and much rain renders them too wet for Sheep.

The myriads of *Geeſe* are incalculable, The whole are ſubjeéted to the operation

i of

of " pulling." They are now (13 September) covered with down, only. The operation, I was informed, is repeated feveral times, in the courfe of the fummer; and found very profitable. They are kept on the " Moor," all winter. In long-continued froft and fnow, they are fed, and, generally, I was told, with Beans.

REMARKS.

FROM this curfory view, of thefe un-appropriated lands, they appear to be of fome confiderable value, in their prefent commonable ftate. But viewing them as being, naturally, grazing and mowing grounds of a fuperior quality; and feeing the uncertainty of feafons in this climate; there can be little doubt of their being capable of affording much greater profit, to individuals, and to the Community, in a ftate of appropriation and divifion.

The prompt objection to the alteration is that of giving a check to the rearing of Cattle; and, fome will add, to the rearing

of

of Geefe. The laft, however, is not an object of fufficient importance, either in RURAL, or POLITICAL ECONOMY, to weigh, as an argument, on this fubject;—though the feathers may be entitled to their full weight. And, with refpect to the former, it may be faid, that it cannot be good policy to fuffer lands to lie in an under-productive ftate; by way of forcing the propagation of any particular fpecies of animals; to the detriment of the aggregate produce of the Country.

CURSORY

CURSORY REMARKS

IN A JOURNEY THROUGH

SOMERSETSHIRE*.

TIVERTON

TO

TAUNTON.

(Twentyone Miles.)

FRIDAY, 19 SEPTEMBER, 1794.

LEAVE the charming environs of Tiverton: the fineſt ſituation in Devonſhire; and one of the firſt in the Iſland.

Meet many lime carts, from the works
on the borders of Somerſetſhire. The lime
moſtly in bags: ſome in bulk.

Pack-

---

* In continuation of that through NORTH DEVON-
SHIRE. I muſt again apologize for the *nakedneſs* of theſe
remarks.

Packhorfes laden with hay, in truffes.

A view of the rich environs of Bradnich opens : backed by the hills of Eaft Devon-fhire.

Pafs through a rich plot of country, round Halbertòn (three miles). The fub-foil red grouty gravel ; as near Hatherley.

Some fields of fine turneps ; beautifully clean.

The road good : now mending, with flinty gravel, or broken flints.

More good turneps ; near Sampford.

A variegated fubfoil : red and white.

Enter flat furzegrown commons, and leave the rich Diftrict of Tiverton.

The Blackdown hills, with mountain features, appear in front, and at hand.

Meet more lime carts, and fome wag-gons : the laft of the Weft of England con-ftruction.

Inftance of mowing dwarf furze : a fecond workman following, with a rake, to form the fwaths into faggots.

Pafs a young plantation of foreft trees, of different fpecies ; put in among dwarf furze : the firft inftance of planting (ex-cepting

cepting the Scotch firs near Hatherley) obferved in this journey of near a hundred
miles !

Pits of red gravel, by the fide of a good
road.

The fubfoil—a feam of waterworn gravel, and rough pebbles.

Leave the Vale of Exeter.

Join the Exeter road (nine miles), and
enter Maiden Down : a wide furzegrown
common : the depreffed ridge which feparates the Vales of Exeter and Taunton.

A broad view of Somerfetfhire breaks
upon the eye : the Vale of Taunton, backed
by the Quantoc hills.

Obferve fmall and very neat cattle, on the
commons.

A deep white fandy fubftratum, and
heavy fandy roads.

Some good oxen of the *Somerfetfhire*
breed. Not fo *clean* as the beft of the
North Devonfhire.

More beautifully clean turneps.

Sandy road, and hollow way : the fubftratum red fandy rock.

A tall

A tall Englifh orchard ! (near Wellington) the ftems five or fix feet high.

Inftance of burning Beat, in the Devonfhire manner.

Weftcountry waggons prevail : no infection.

A fallow laid up, in ribs and trenches,

Poor village huts.

Six oxen ftirring a fallow of ftrong red land.

Meet a ftring of culm carts ; on their way, from the Taunton Navigation, to the Limeworks.

Some neat clean young cattle.

Dip into a clofe wood-bound flat : high hedges and hedgerow timber ; as in Eaft Norfolk.

The hedgebanks lower ; but ftill wide, and partake of the Devonfhire coppice hedges.

Devonfhire tools in ufe, here. The pointed fhovel, common.

Pafs feveral pieces of good clean turneps.

Hedge trees univerfally lopped.

A few

A few fingle Hawthorn hedges begin to appear.

Several inftances of ftubble turneps.

Some thick polled fheep.

Lime compoft, on headlands, as in Devonfhire.

Inftance of bean ftubble, or the " arrifh" of fome other pulfe, dunged for wheat.

Some good Somerfetfhire oxen: dark blood red.

Subfoil variegated: ftreaks of red and white.

Healthy, tallftemed, Englifh orchards.

Leave the red land: the foil and fubfoil, now, of a light brown color.

Obferve fmall mountain fheep; partially horned; as thofe of Okehampton.

Much hedgerow timber; moftly Elm.

A dairy of good cows.

Charming road; with a high broad footpath. A London-like approach to

TAUNTON;—a large, well built, handfome town: the tower of the Church of St. Mary is fingularly tall and beautiful.

THE

The Market of Taunton.

THE Market Place of Taunton is one of the firſt in the Kingdom ; whether as to ſize, neatneſs, or accommodations : a triangular incloſure, fitted up with ſtreets of covered ſtalls, for butchers meat, and furniſhed with ſpacious colonnades, for corn, poultry, &c. and one for cheeſe, bacon, and other articles,—which are ſold, *retail,* by farmers' wives and daughters : an unuſual, but a very *political* way of bringing theſe articles, at once, to the conſumer ; without the intervention of mere dealers.

The Corn Market, here, as in Norfolk, is held in the afternoon ; beginning about three o'clock.   Much corn in the market, in narrow two buſhel bags ; each ſeller having a tray, to ſhoot part of a bag into, that its quality may be the better ſeen. Obſerved no ſamples ; but underſtand that much is ſold through their medium *

TAUNTON

---

* Theſe Remarks, on the Market of Taunton, were chiefly made in 1791.

T A U N T O N

T O

S O M E R T O N.

(Eighteen Miles.)

SATURDAY, 20 SEPTEMBER, 1794.

THE Country, for the firſt two miles, is nearly flat : then ſomewhat ſwelling : a rich fine country.

Hawthorn hedges common.

Many ſtubble turneps : ſome of them promiſing.

Much arable land : ſoil moſtly a ſtrong red loam.

Many wheat ſtubbles turned under : an evidence of the forward ſtate of huſbandry.

Arriſh mows common, in this part of Somerſetſhire.

Inſtance of an Ox cart, with the yoke hung to the pole, by means of a wooden bow, inſtead of an iron ring. Doubtleſs

the

the primitive method. Beautifully fimple; but liable to accidents.

Mifletoe obfervable in the orchards!

The plow of Somerfetfhire has a long but well turned moldboard; with a wreft, ftanding fomewhat high : and with a ladder-piece behind, which fteadies a long, flender, right handle, fhooting forward to the beam.

Leave a plot of vale land, to the right.

The under ftratum appears in feams of red earth, and a fort of white ftoney fubftance.

Wheat ftubbles in narrow ridges, as throughout Devonfhire.

Many fallows, for wheat, are feen.

Act of Parliament hedges, againft the road. The firft, probably, of any extent, from the Landsend.

Still many hedgerow Elms.

Inftance of paring and burning.

A large field orchard going to decay

Pafs fome good young cattle.

The pointed fhovel ftill in ufe.

Crofs a dip of cold weak land (five miles)

A rainy

A rainy ſtormy morning. How convenient is a carriage, and how productive of
information ! A tablet full of intereſting
facts, in travelling five or ſix miles ; notwithſtanding the unfavorableneſs of the
morning. A traveller on horſeback could
not look up: nor if anything met his eye,
could he note it, with conveniency *.

Ox carts (wains or coops) common.

Inſtance of a young field orchard (at
North Curry). The plants tall, and ſet
out at good diſtances, in the beſt Herefordſhire manner.

A quarry of blue building ſtone.

Many orchard grounds.

A newly planted quickſet hedge.

Many neat young cattle.

The ſoil and ſubſoil ſtill red.

Good limeſtone road †.

VOL. II.　　O　　　Aſcend

---

* This remark applies to TRAVELLING. In examining a particular Diſtrict or STATION, RIDING ON
HORSEBACK is preferable to a carriage ; and WALKING,
infinitely preferable to either.

† A ſingular method of breaking road materials, eſpecially the baſe flints, that have been repeatedly mentioned,
is

Afcend the limeftone heights *.

Carts and waggons, at the lime kilns: no pack horfes.

A good back view of the Vale of Taunton.

A broad view of South Sedgemore,— covered with cattle, fheep, and geefe; and, over it, a view of the Poldown and Mendip hills.

Some good horned lambs.

Thin limeftone land; and more lime kilns.

A rich looking valley of land opens to the right.

Inftance of a field orchard, in a ftate of arable culture, as in Herefordfhire.

A Sedgemore, or Marfh, of fome extent, is feen to the right.

Swing plows univerfal.

More field orchards.

The hedges of the road cropped.

A herd

is obfervable in this Country: a one-handed hammer being ufed, by a workman fitting: a method which, it is afferted, is more expeditious, than the ordinary one of ufing the fledge hammer.

* See Page 176.

A herd of tall thin white pigs.

Continue upon cold limeſtone heights.

Paſs Burton Pynſent.

A neat farmery, and large farm.

Clean fallows, and good clover.

Farm hedges kept down to fence height.

Four heavy horſes plowing broken ground.

Six oxen employed in the ſame operation; with heavy long ſwing plows.

A full hedgerow of apple trees; as about Bromyard in Herefordſhire.

Paſs through Curry Rival.

Strong cold land: wheat, beans, and clover.

See large flocks of horned ſheep; of a breed ſimilar to that of Dorſetſhire and Eaſt Devonſhire.

Leave the limeſtone heights, and deſcend towards Langport.

A wide Vale Diſtrict opens to the right.

A naked Chiltern Country, in front, and to the left.

Six oxen at plow, and four at harrow: all in yoke: alſo two at plow, with two horſes before them; as in the South Hams

of Devonſhire; and as formerly in Yorkſhire.

See Ham Hill, or Hamdown Hill; a
broken prominent, ſtriking object.

Flat-roofed hayricks, as in Cleveland.

Croſs the Parret, at LANGPORT,—a
mean market town. A Navigation and
Coal Yard.

Pantiles in uſe, as a covering.

Enter a common field: the firſt from
the Landsend.

Foul bad huſbandry: couch and thiſtles.

The ſubſoil limeſtone gravel; yet the
land appears to be cold and weak.

Flocks of ſheep now in theſe open fields.

Another flat of marſhes appear to the
right.

In front; a wide range of limeſtone
Downs. Large depreſſed ſwells of arable
lands, with ſhallow graſſy dips between
them: part in open common fields,—part
incloſed.

A windmill appears: the firſt in this
journey.

Large flocks of ſheep, in the open fields.

A ſheep fold: the firſt.

An

An open naked Cambridgeſhire-like Country.

Catch a diſtant view of the Dorſetſhire hills.

Many good cart horſes, on the road.

Large limeſtone flags—or coarſe marble ſlabs—raiſed near the road.

The plow team—four horſes, at length.

The tops of the ſwells are dry—ſtone to the ſurface : but the ſides appear cold and weak.

Foul thiſtly common fields.

A roughly broken paſſage, to the left.

A large ſheep fold.

Somerton appears in a broad flat ; or ſhallow baſon ; with riſing grounds on every ſide.

A large field of rough old graſsland : *appropriated waſte.*

An ox waggon, partially loaded with ſtraw, and thatched : doubtleſs, a harveſt waggon, thus ſet by for the next ſeaſon.

Enter SOMERTON,—another mean market town : the ſuburbs in ruins.

SOMERTON

AND ITS

ENVIRONS.

A DECAYING Place: the remains, probably, of a good Town: now, evidently, in neglect.

The building materials limeſtone and thatch. The ſtones neatly formed, as in the Vale of Pickering.

Below the Town, towards the Eaſt, the environs are beautifully broken. A valley of rich marſh land, overlooked by bold wooded knolls.

Large good oxen, and good, horned wedders, now grazing in the marſhes.

SOMERTON

TO

SHIPTON MALLET.

(Fifteen Miles.)

SATURDAY, 20 SEPTEMBER, 1794.

CROSS the meadowy valley, and wind among the rugged hillocks, which form its Northern bank.

A flock

A flock of very neat, horned ewes:—
in the beſt *Dorſetſhire* form.

Aſcend a thin ſoiled limeſtone ſwell.

The Valley re-opens, to the right.

Paſs a dairy of indifferent cows.

The ſoil enereaſes in ſtrength.

Small fields and hedgerow elms: evi-
dences of deep well ſoiled land; but unuſual
in elevated ſituations.

The Country now more open; and a
fine Valley is diſcloſed to the left.

A remarkable line of road; on a well
ſoiled ridge, with a rich Vale Diſtrict, on
either hand: the Vallies of Somerton and
Glaſtonbury.

The conical hillock, near Glaſtonbury,
ſurmounted by a tower, is a ſtriking object, in this point of view.

Strong wheat ſtubbles, on theſe uplands.

A fallow for wheat, now folding.

Marble quarries on either ſide of the
road. Many men at work; and teams
waiting. Moſtly raiſed in large ſlabs, ſix
or eight inches thick, and ſeveral feet in
dimenſions. Lie horizontally, and near the

ſurface

furface of level ground.   Men employed in polifhing them.   The color a blue grey.

Village buildings of ftone and pantile.

Some orchards, on this cool foil.   But the fubftratum is calcareous.

The Valley or Vale of Glaftonbury, backed by the Mendip Hills, fpreads wide beneath the eye.

Enter cold-foiled common fields (five miles).

Beans a prevailing crop.

The foil a cold crumbling clay; like that over the clayftone of the Vale of Glocefter.

Reach the point of the cold-foiled ridge; and defcend into the VALE OF GLASTON-BURY *.

Crofs the river Brent, at Lydford.

A parcel of ill formed cows, moftly black.

Cold Vale land—at prefent bare of herbage.

The

* This is a difficult paffage of country to clafs.   It is more than a *Valley*; yet wants fomething of the *Vale* character.   However, below the part, here croffed, it feems to fpread wider, and to acquire a variety of outline and diverfity of furface.   I denominate it of Glaftonbury, as it contains that antient place.

The mile ſtones ſhamefully defaced; but how eaſy to remedy the defeɛt, with paint.

Marble ſtiles and fences common.

Elm trees and pollards, ſcattered over graſs incloſures.

Still a cold flat Vale Diſtriɛt. The fields blue, with Devilsbit (*Scabioſa ſuccifa*).

The graſs incloſures interſeɛted with ſurface drains. A very cold plot of country: weak and languid, even at this ſeaſon of the year. Adapted to the cheeſe dairy, and the rearing of cattle.

Some lean cows: but of a better breed than the laſt.

Many pollards in the hedges.

A plot of woodland, well timbered: much of the land of this Vale is well adapted to oak timber. The hedgerows, at leaſt, ought to be filled with it.

The whole in a ſtate of graſs: no arable land ſeen from the road.

Another dairy of ſmall ill formed cows.

Hayſtacks in the field; as in the dairy Diſtriɛts of Yorkſhire.

The land improves: ſtill wholly in graſs.

A well-

A well foiled rifing ground, in front; wholly covered with grafs.

A large dairy of cows, of the middle-horned breed; but not of the *Devonfhire* variety.

Hayftacks capped, only, with thatch; as in the Yorkfhire practice.

Some roomy good cows: varioufly colored?

Arrive at the foot of the hill: the Vale is fome three or four miles wide.

The road acrofs it is a ftraight line. Q. Roman?

Another dairy of many colored cows.

Reach the upper ftages of the fteep;— and enjoy the views:—extenfive, rich, and picturable.

Good grafsland upon thefe hills; and ftocked with good cows.

From the fummit of the hill, an entire circle of views are commanded: a wide fea of grafslands: the hills and the Vale equally green.

The fubfoil, of this fertile upland, is limeftone gravel, in thin layers, between loam.

Some

Some very good cows, on thefe hills.

Another Vale opens to the left : a fine, ftrongly featured country.

A large Marfh or Sedgemore appears to the left.

Obferve feveral *fheet cows :* are they natives of Somerfetfhire * ?

Many good fheep,—of the Dorfetfhire, or Weft of England breed.   They appear to be common to Dorfetfhire, Eaft Devon-fhire, and this part of Somerfetfhire.

A rick frame loaded with ftraw, and thatched as a roof.

Meet a load of *Somerfetfhire* " reed :" differing from that of *Devonfhire*; as having the ears cut off : confifting of clean ftraight unbruifed ftems only.

Defcend into another Valley of grafsland : narrower, but better foiled, than the laft.

Limeftone ftill raifed by the fide of the road :

* This fingular variety, which is obfervable in Gentle-men's grounds, in different parts of the Ifland, is given by color, chiefly or wholly.   A SHEET COW refembles a red cow of North Devonfhire, or Weft Somerfetfhire, with a white fheet thrown over her barrel; her head, neck, fhoulders, and hind parts, being uncovered.

road : thick ſtrata of brown earth between the ſeams of ſtone ; differing from the blue marble.

Inſtance of underdraining, with flat ſtones ſet up, in the form of the letter V, inverted.

Aſcend another range of graſsland ſwells.

Stone fence walls, on theſe uplands : the firſt, from the weſtward, in this line of road. Some, in courſes of dry ſtones, alternately with other courſes, laid in earth mortar.

Inſtance of unbitten aftergraſs ; the firſt obſerved, in this ſtage :—a dairy country.

Good horned wedders, in theſe graſs grounds.

Leave a rich graſſy hillock, to the right.

The valley of Shipton opens prettily·:--- rich graſsland, beautifully ſurfaced ; but disfigured with ſtone fences.

SHIPTON

SHIPTON

AND ITS

ENVIRONS.

A SMALL Market Town; fituated near the head of a fine valley.

The church ftately, and in a good ftyle of architecture. Several neat houfes: a feat of the woollen manufacture.

On the North fide of the valley, are fome bold hillocks, compofed wholly of maffes of limeftone, covered with a rich deep foil. The rock remarkably ftrong: very different from the blue marble, before noticed. This, in general appearance, refembles more the ftone of St. Vincent's rock, near Briftol.

A limekiln and large quarries;—feemingly of long ftanding.

Afhen pollards fcattered over thefe grafslands; chiefly by the fides of ftone walls: a practice I have elfewhere obferved, on well foiled limeftone lands.

Some confiderable dairies of good cows, in thefe environs.

SHIPTON

SHIPTON MALLET

T O

F R O M E.

(Twelve Miles)

SUNDAY, 21 SEPTEMBER, 1794.

CROSS the valley above the town: the water a mere rivulet. No appearance of mills of manufacture.

A shameful road toll: and this where materials are so abundant.

Pass a dairy of twenty or thirty good cows.

A large flock of sheep, on a thinsoiled hillock to the right.

Rise another grassy height: the soil redish; the subsoil limestone gravel.

A foul wheat stubble; and an attempt at turneps. Dairy men are bad arable farmers.

More

More large light-colored cows; alfo a few calves: the firft obferved in this cow Diftrict!

More finch-backed, Glocefterfhire-like cows: with fome mixed-breed heifers. how little young ftock appears.

A wide view, to the right,, backed by the broken heights of Stourton.

Still grafsland and afhen pollards: with fome ftone fences; but more thorn hedges.

Pafs fome large dairy farm.

A herd of good Weft of England cows: a fingle inftance.

A limeftone quarry: a ftrong redifh rock: the foil over it red, and of good depth.

Leave the limeftone grafsland Country.

Enter a weakfoiled arable Diftrict: the *foil* ftill red: in appearance, the fame as that which covers the limeftone rock.

The foil ftill weaker: fandy and wet.

A ftrongly featured country to the right; about Stourton.

A wide Vale Diftrict opens, in front. The fertile Vale of Trowbridge: fkreened, on the right, by the Wiltfhire Downs; and,

and, on the left, by the diftant hills of Gloceſterſhire; with the broad Vale of North Wiltſhire winding in between them.

Defcend into another grafsland dairy Diſtrict.

Large mottled cows: fomewhat of the ſhort-horned appearance: a few of their horns ſhooting forward and dipping at the points!

The Warminſter Hills appear at hand.

The fubfoil, again, a limeſtone rubble.

Good hawthorn hedges.

Wheat already in a green, grafſy ſtate!

Leave a woodland valley, to the right (fix miles).

More wheat, in Weſt of England ridges.

The towered height of Stourton forms a prominent feature.

Drop into a broken wooded Vale Diſtrict; the head of the Valley of Frome.

Grafsland — and dairy cows; — of the middle-horned breed, and the finch-backed variety.

Hayſtacks in the ſhape of dumplins, or inverted turneps, as in Cleyeland.

Round

Round rodden cow cribs, as in Glocefter-fhire.

A fmall orchard or two.

Large dairy grounds, intermixed with arable inclofures.

A flock of good Wiltfhire ewes.

Crofs a fweetly wooded dell.

The fubftratum, on the weft fide, red fhattered rock; on the eaft fide, pale foft rubble: diftinct maffes of materials.

Village Buildings — ftone pantiles and thatch; with fome heavy ftone-flates.

Pafs a large farmery, on the right.

A paffage of fine grafsland.

Good ftone road, between cropped hedges.

Enter FROME: a large well built place; in a fine fituation. Several neat boxes, in its environs: the town likewife neat; though a manufacturing place: — Leeds, without its coals and dirt. The Warminfter and Longleat Hills, are good objects from thefe environs.

F R O M E

T o

D E V I Z E S.

(Twenty Miles)

SUNDAY, 21 SEPTEMBER, 1794.

MORE deep loam on limeſtone : with mixed cultivation : graſs and arable.

Stone walls, in the environs of Frome, as of Shipton : ugly, it is true ; but effectual againſt hedgebreakers. Both of them are manufacturing towns ; and, of courſe, inhabited, by the diſſolute and daring.

A large dairy of longiſh-horned cows : apparently of a mixed breed.

A rich, clean country (two miles).

The name of the village, on a board, at the entrance of " Beckington :" a liberal act, in thoſe who placed it there.

A large

A large dairy of mixed cows.

The road hedges legally kept.

Field hay ricks ftill common.

Three full-bred longhorned cows: the firft.

Deep clayey fubfoil (four miles).

Single-wheeled plows, with winding wooden moldboards.

A recent inclofure, from a ftate of common.

The land a deep loam. The quickfets guarded with two lines of dead hedgework.

A flat, yet apparently, dry country.

Enter WILTSHIRE.

A cold flat vale paffage.

Farm houfes—of timber and brick pannels; with weatherboarded barns; as in the Southern Counties.

Rife a dryer, betterfoiled fwell of land: Stocked with large herds of cows.

Fat cart horfes, at grafs (Sunday).

A view of North Wiltfhire opens, in front.

Longhorned Cows, and Weft of England Oxen.

Pafs through Trowbridge; a fair town, finely fituated. Many good houfes. The principal ftreet is remarkably neat. Seated on-a clean fwell of rich land; overlooking a fweetly wooded bafon, backed by the Wiltfhire Hills.

Catch a broad and extenfive view of the Vale of North Wiltfhire.

The road hedges univerfally fhorn.

Inftance of high grafsland ridges, as in Glocefterfhire and North Wiltfhire: the firft obferved in this journey.

Some large orchard grounds.

Bad roads: foft limeftone is among the worft of road materials.

Many hedgerow Ellms.

Singlewheel plows, in common ufe.

Some very foul bad farming:

And a large inclofure of rough anthilly land: left, in this wafteful ftate,—as if to keep the arable lands in countenance.

Gates, with four bars, and fhouldered hartrees, univerfal, acrofs this Vale.

Twenty full-bred longhorned cows.

A fine Vale Diftrict: rich *waves* of grafs-land (3 miles from Trowbridge).

More

More rich grafslands; ftocked with longhorned cows: now apparently in full poffeffion.

Many hedgerow Elms: fome of them large.

A compleat dairy country (three to four miles). A fmall goofe and pig common: how much like many paffages of the Vales of Glocefterfhire.

A good longhorned bull; and fome heifers.

See, in a quarry, fine loam, three feet deep, on limeftone!

Some patches of field potatoes.

A wide extent of Elm-wooded Vale, to the right.

Many good Wiltfhire fheep.

The bafe, or unbroken area, of the Vale terminates. Afcend the fair hillock of Seend: --- charming fituation! rich and beautiful views, from every point: three or four habitable houfes fcattered on the hill: elegant village!

Crofs a dip of rich arable land: ftrong dark brown foil. Wheat and beans; but no clover!

P 3   Afcend

Afcend the firſt ſtage of the Wiltſhire Hills, to Devizes; a large and reſpectable market town; finely ſituated.

From its environs, catch a broad view of the rich and extenſive Vale of Trowbridge; backed by the riſing grounds of Somerſet-ſhire, and diſtanced by the Mendip Hills;— tracing back, with the eye, a principal part of this day's journey.

A GENERAL

A

GENERAL VIEW

OF THE

MORE SOUTHERN PARTS

OF

SOMERSETSHIRE.

THE Line of Country, which paffed more immediately under the eye, in this journey, varies much, in Natural Characters, and Rural Management; feparating, analytically, into

The Vale of Taunton;

The inclofed Limeftone Heights, between the Tone and the Parret;

The open-Field Diftrict, or Limeftone Downs, between Langport and Somerton:

The ftrong arable Lands, on Limeftone, between the Brook of Somerton and the Brent;

The Vale of Glaftonbury;

P 4　　　　The

The rich Grafsland Limeſtone Heights on either ſide of Shipton Mallet; terminating in

The Vale of Trowbridge.

The ELEVATION of this Line of Country is inconſiderable; unleſs towards its Eaſtern extremity. The tide flows, or has heretofore flowed, within much of theſe Southern parts of Somerſetſhire; extenſive flats of marſhes being ſeen on either hand. About Shipton, and thence towards Frome, the ground riſes, but not conſiderably, and the waters which fall on it divide; part of them paſſing weſtward to the Bay of Bridgewater; the reſt falling into the branches of the Avon.

The SURFACE is ſingularly diverſified; the hills frequently riſe abruptly, from wide flat vallies, or extenſive tracts of marſhes, which ſpread their broad level ſurfaces between them; giving them, in ſome points of view, and through a humid atmoſphere, the appearance of Iſlands.

The CLIMATURE is probably forward. Every appearance of harveſt had paſſed away

The

The WATERS,---SOILS,---SUBSOILS,---
and FOSSILS, are detailed in the Journal;
and it may be needlefs to remark, here,
that, between the Vales of Taunton and
Trowbridge (both of which have evidently
been formed, with heterogeneous materials),
the Country is a continued chain of LIME-
STONE hills; or that the nature of the
ftone is ftrikingly different; confifting of
two diftinct fpecies of Limeftone; which
doubtlefs have had feparate origins; the
wide Valley of Glaftonbury appearing to
divide them.

The INLAND NAVIGATIONS, obferved,
are thofe of Taunton and Langport. Few
parts of this Ifland are better adapted to
navigable Canals, than this part of Somerfetfhire: and furely, the Brent and the
Avon, feeing the Coals, the Limeftone, and
the Manufacture, which lie between them,
might be joined with advantage.

The STATE OF INCLOSURE appears in
the detail: the entire Country is inclofed;
except the moors or common marfhes, and
the paffage of open common fields, between
Langport and Somerton.

The

The PRODUCTIONS may likewiſe be gathered from the detail. ˙ To the Weſt of the Valley of Glaſtonbury, *arable crops* are prevalent : in that Vale, and to the Eaſt of it, *graſsland* is the almoſt only produce, even to the confines of the County, and through the whole of the Vale of Trowbridge : an extent of graſsland Country, which is rarely met with ; eſpecially where the ſurface is greatly diverſified. Of *woodland*, this Line of Country, the Vales which terminate it excepted, may be ſaid to be deſtitute : and the *hedgerow wood* is inconſiderable ; the fuel being chiefly, perhaps, *peats* of the fens and marſhes.

VILLAGE and FARM BUILDINGS are wholly of ſtone, covered with thatch, tiles, or a heavy kind of ſlate. Left the mud wall, in the Vale of Taunton ; and met the half-timber building, and weatherboarding, in the Vale of Trowbridge.

A BROAD CLOTH MANUFACTURE, of conſiderable extent, I believe, is carried on, in the Eaſtern parts of this Line of Country. But, in travelling it, few traces of ſuch a manufacture appear. The manufacturing

Diſtricts

Diftricts of Yorkfhire, and Lancafhire,—
more efpecially thofe of the woolen manufactures, are marked by their dirt and
mifery: companions, however, which, it
would appear, in travelling through Somerfetfhire and Wiltfhire, are not effentially
neceffary to the WOOLEN MANUFACTURE:
the moft NATURAL, as well as the moft
POLITICAL, branch of Manufacture, this
Ifland can encourage.

The FARMS, or parcels of land in the
occupation of individuals, appear to be
fmall; efpecially the arable farms, on the
Weft fide of the County, where the life-
leafe tenure is prevalent, and extends, I
believe, more or lefs throughout the county
of Somerfet, and within that of Wilts.
On the Eaft fide of the County, there appears to be fome dairy farms of a greater
magnitude.

BEASTS OF LABOR. On the arable fide
of the County, Oxen are prevalent, and
freely ufed, in all the ordinary works of
hufbandry; but, in the dairy country, and
on the borders of Wiltfhire, a lefs *profitable*
race

race of animals (for the Public at leaft) is,
I fear, in common.ufe *

The CATTLE of Somerfetfhire are various. The Weft of England breed are
confined to the Weftern and Southern parts
of the County; the Vale of Glaftonbury
appearing,

* TAX ON HORSES. In thefe days of famine and
taxation,—what political blindnefs muft that be, which
fuffers the produce of the Country to be confumed, by
animals that make no return to the magazine of human
food; nor make any adequate recompenfe to the Community,
for the expence they are hourly creating. Animals that
are preying on the fuftinence which is wanted to fupprefs the
cravings of the fpecies. Animals for whofe fupport the
Country may be faid to be now paying fums incalculable.
And, furely, they ought to be made accountable for an
adequate part of the debt they are lavifhly incurring.

A tax of one Guinea, a year (on every horfe, whether
ufed in hufbandry or otherwife), for the firft three years,
with an additional tax of one Guinea, a year, every third
year, fo long as found policy fhall fee right (thus allowing
time for the rearing of cattle), will raife an immenfe
revenue; will leffen, effentially, the confumption of grain;
and throw into the markets an abundant increafe of
animal food.

For Remarks, and Calculations, on the comparative
Effect of Horfes and Cattle, as Beafts of Draft in
Hufbandry, fee the RURAL ECONOMY of the MIDLAND
COUNTIES, Vol. I. Page 470.

appearing, in the Line of Country travelled through in this journey, to be the Northern boundary of this breed. The cows of the dairy Diftrict are probably bought in ; many of them have the marks of the Glocefterfhire breed ; while others wear appearances of the middle-horned breed of the North of Yorkfhire :---light colored, and irregularly pied : a variety of color in the middle-horned breed, which I did not expect to have met with, in Somerfetfhire. Knowing that the long-horned breed have been for a length of time eftablifhed in North Wiltfhire, and the red breed in the Vale of Taunton, I expected to have found a mixture of thefe two breeds, rather than a diftinct variety.

The SHEEP of Somerfetfhire have not been lefs the fubject of furprize, than its cattle. I did not expect to find what in Smithfield is emphatically called " horned fheep,"--- and much lefs the *Dorfetfhire* variety of that fort,---inhabiting, as a native breed, any part of Somerfetfhire. But perhaps they are moft prevalent, in Somerfetfhire.

fetſhire, as in Devonſhire, on the Dorſet-ſhire ſide of the County.

Of SWINE,: Somerſetſhire appears ſtill to perſevere in the old white breed ; which may be ſaid to be in full poſſeſſion of the more Weſtern Counties.

Of BEES I *obſerved* but one ſolitary hive ! In the long Line of Country, between Cornwall and Wiltſhire, I do not recollect to have *ſeen* more than half a dozen of thoſe induſtrious families ! --- whoſe labors are clear gain to a Country,---who contribute to the National ſtock without diminiſhing any other article of its produce.

A RETROSPECTIVE

A

RETROSPECTIVE VIEW

OF THE

WEST OF ENGLAND.

FROM the foregoing Examinations, it is evident, that the Point of Land, which is the more immediate fubject of thefe Volumes, forms a NATURAL DE-PARTMENT of this Kingdom; and that it was, heretofore (and ftill indeed may be faid to remain), a PENINSULA,---partially cut off, by inlets of the Bays of Bridgewater and Bridport, from the main body of the Ifland.

It is equally evident, from thefe furveys, that the Department now in view is, at prefent, under a courfe of RURAL MA-NAGEMENT which differs, in many refpects,

from

from that of the Ifland at large ; and whofe
bafis, it is highly probable, has had a feparate origin.

Judging from the modern practice of
colonization, it is reafonable to fuppofe,
that the Bays, Inlets, and Eftuaries of
Rivers, in this Ifland, were the firft fettled ;
and that, as inhabitants encreafed, cultivation, by progreffive fteps, approached
the higher lands ; climbing, in the courfe
of time, to the interior heights.

Admitting that Cornwall and Devonfhire
were early colonized, and the whole of
them by the fame people ; and that, afterward, a colony of a different race, took
poffeffion of the inlets of the Bay of Bridgewater, and the rich and ample fhores, which,
at that time, they doubtlefs afforded, the
differences that are now obfervable, in the
Rural Practices of their defcendants, may
be, with lefs difficulty, reconciled.

On this principle of colonization, the
Vale of Taunton,—had the time of fettlement (or invafion) been the fame,—would
naturally

naturally have belonged to the settlers (or invaders) of the Bay of Bridgewater; but admitting, what will not I believe be doubted, that the Vale of Exeter was priorly possessed, and that its inhabitants had over-topped the depressed ridge which divides these Vales, before their Northern neigh-bours had approached it, the VALE OF TAUNTON would, in course, fall into the hands of the first settlers; and the same circumstances would naturally attend the range of heights, and their Northeastern skirts, which form what I have here named the DAIRY DISTRICT.

In process of time, and when the entire Country became subject to the same Go-vernment, a mixture of practices would take place, and the two established systems of Management would mix, and blend with each other, in the manner in which we find them, at the present day.

The Practices which, now, more parti-cularly distinguish what, for the sake of perspicuity, I have denominated the DAN-MONIAN HUSBANDRY,---will appear in

VOL. II.   Q   the

the following detail : some particulars of which, however, are common to the four most Western Counties ; as if they had once been politically united ; with customs distinct from those of the rest of the Island : the particulars, here alluded to, relating to matters of *Policy*, rather than to *Agriculture*.

The CULTIVAT-ION OF COMMONABLE LANDS is, I believe, peculiar to this extremity of the Island.

The LIFE-LEASEHOLD TENURE, though not peculiar to the West of England, is the most prevalent within it.

The uniform prevalency of SMALL FARMS mark it, in a similar manner.

The singular MANAGEMENT OF COPPICE WOOD, which has been described, is common, and perhaps peculiar, to the Department in view.

The extraordinary FENCES of this part of the Island mark it most discriminately— common and peculiar to the Peninsula ! even to this day ! !

EARTHEN WALLS, though not peculiar to the West of England, is in no other
quarter

quarter of the Ifland, carried up fo high, and fo fubftantially, as in this.

The circumftance of having no fixed places of hiring, or ftated times of changing, FARM SERVANTS, is, I believe, peculiar to the more Weftern Counties.

The practice of putting out the children of paupers to farmers, as APPRENTICES IN HUSBANDRY, is, as an eftablifhed cuftom likewife, peculiar to this part of the Ifland.

That of performing CARRIAGE ON HORSEBACK, may now be faid to belong to this extreme part of the Ifland, only. Even in the Highlands of Scotland, it is in a manner laid afide.

Many or moft of the IMPLEMENTS and TOOLS of this Peninfula are peculiar to it.

The practice of BURNING BEAT (by velling, harrowing, &c.), for wheat and turneps, is likewife peculiar to this Peninfula.

In the MANAGEMENT OF LIME—as in feparating the ftones and afhes; mixing it with earth; as well as the manner of

Q 2   fpreading

ſpreading it on the land,---this part of the Iſland differs widely from the reſt.

In the HARVEST MANAGEMENT, we meet with many ſingular traits of practice. The Arriſh Mow appears to be common to the Peninſula,---even to its outſkirts.

HOUSING STACKS, by hand, though petty, is peculiar.   And WINNOWING, in the open air, though once, doubtleſs, the univerſal practice, is now peculiar to Devonſhire and Cornwall ; I mean, as the prevailing practice of an extenſive, well ſoiled, cultivated Country.

The method of THRASHING WHEAT, without bruiſing the ſtraw, is peculiar to the more Weſtern Counties : with, however, a notable difference that has been mentioned *.

In the Management of particular Crops, the SOWING OF WHEAT is the moſt remarkable.   But the CULTURE OF TURNEPS may, at this day, be conſidered as almoſt equally extraordinary.

The TEMPORARY LEY, of five or ſix years, though not peculiar to this Penin
ſula ;

* See Page 203.

fula; yet marks it, very difcriminately, from the other Weſtern and Southern Counties.

WATERING THE SLOPES OF. HILLS, though not uncommon, at preſent; yet, a century ago, it was probably confined to this point of the Iſland; and is, at this time, nowhere elſe ſo prevalent.

By its ORCHARD GROUNDS, this Department of the Iſland is moſt difcriminately marked.

By the purity of its Breed of CATTLE, which though not *ſpecifically* peculiar to this Department, are evidently a diſtinct *Variety*; which, in all human probability, have deſcended, lineally, and without admixture, from the native breed.

The fatting of GRASS CALVES, though not peculiar to this part of the Iſland, being likewiſe common in Norfolk, may neverthelefs be confidered as a diſtinct practice; as, in the interſpace of two hundred miles, which ſeparates them, I have not obſerved it, in the ordinary practice of Farmers.

The

The fingular method of RAISING CREAM, which is practifed in this Country, may be called its own.

The BLEEDING of grown CATTLE, for the SLAUGHTER, I have not met·with, out of this Department.

The practice of keeping SWINE to two or three years old, and the method of fatting them, are peculiar to this Country. That of boiling their food, and of letting all the females remain in a ftate of fecundity, may likewife be mentioned as peculiarities.

The Mountain SHEEP of this part of the Ifland, appear to be peculiar to it. Thofe of the Mendip Hills I have not had an opportunity of examining.

In the SHEPHERDING of fheep, we have feen fome ftriking traits of practice

And the practice of SHEARING fheep, without previoufly WASHING their wool, is at prefent peculiar to a part of this Peninfula.

In this detail of peculiarities, we find many which cannot owe their origin to the

firft

firſt civilized poſſeſſors. But what ſtrikes us moſt forcibly, in examining it, is, that in the lapſe of centuries, its Rural Practices ſhould not have aſſimilated, more freely, with thoſe of the Iſland at large.

MINUTES

IN

WEST DEVONSHIRE.

INTRODUCTORY REMARKS.

THE EXTEMPORARY OBSER-
VATIONS, that are here offered,
may be confidered as a continuation of
thofe, which occurred in my PRACTICE,
in SURREY, in NORFOLK, and in the
MIDLAND DISTRICT.

If thefe which I am now offering, and
with the fame facrifice of feelings that has
ever attended my publication of extemporary Memoranda, have any claim to peculiarity of character, it confifts in their

pointing,

pointing out the regular approach to the Field of Improvement, and the requifite cautions obfervable, in entering it ; fo as to be able to pafs through it, with fafety and advantage.

In this aggregate capacity, it is prefumed, they may be found ufeful to thofe who are defirous to enter a field, in which forefight and circumfpection are, in a fuperior degree, requifite. Their individual claims I prefume not to adjuft.

MINUTES.

MINUTES.

I.

1791. JULY 14th. FROM PLYMOUTH to BUCKLAND PLACE. Three or four miles from the Town of Plymouth, the fertile inclofed lands of its environs terminate; the traveller entering, apparently, the outfkirts of Dartmore. To the right, wild furze-grown Commons and wooded Vallies are feen; to the left, upland Inclofures. In diftance,—the ragged Tors of Dartmore on the one hand, the Cornifh Mountains on the other: the fcenery truly mountainous; the Valley of the Tamer, and a cultivated dip to the right, being overlooked, and in a great meafure hid from the view.

About feven miles from Plymouth, the Valley of the Tavey opens; and the road, extremely unlevel, dips down to BUCK-

LAND

LAND PLACE; fituated fomewhat below the midway of the flope; at the head of a "Coomb," or inferior Valley; in this cafe fhallow, and fpreading wide as it defcends.

The fituation is naturally reclufe, and is now rendered truly fo, by long negleɛt. The remains of the Priory is the prefent habitation; and has been a refidence of the FAMILY OF DRAKE, from the time of the CIRCUMNAVIGATOR, who purchafed it.

Some half century ago, much planting has been done, round the fite of the Monaftery; and, during the laft twenty or thirty years, fcarcely a bough has been touched. The tower of the Priory, with a monaftic barn of extraordinary fize, and with various Gothic buildings, the remaining Offices of the Monaftery, are feen (in the immediate approach through a grove of trees which fill the head of the Valley with a fullen gloom), as in a foreft, far diftant from the haunts of men.

2.

July 14. Rode over the DEMESNE
LANDS of BUCKLAND PLACE. The
buildings are befet on every fide with
tall groves (and fome of them overhung
with large-grown trees, which are injurious
to their roofs, and liable to crufh them in
their fall), except on the lower fide, to the
Weft, where the Valley is choaked up with
fruit trees, for fome diftance below the
houfe; which is thus involved continually
in a damp and ftagnant air; unfit for men
or animals to breathe. An over ftocked
rookery, which occupies a confiderable part
of thefe groves, is rendered, by this clofe
atmofphere, offenfive in the extreme.

But, burfting from this gloom, one of the
firft farms in the Ifland is entered. It contains near eight hundred acres of land:
lying on every fide of the houfe; but
chiefly

BUCKLAND
FARM.

chiefly below it. Almoſt five hundred acres (including hedges, &c.) are in cultivation ; the reſt in old woodlands, groves, and orchard grounds.

Near thirty acres of the lower grounds of the Valley, over, which a principal part of the cultivated lands are ſpread, have long been imperfectly watered, by a rill that riſes in the uppermoſt part of the farm, and falls down the Valley into the Tavey ; which forms the Weſtern boundary of the farm, for more than a mile.

The upper part of the Valley of the Tavey is a ſteepſided dell ; hung with wood on either ſide ; having a narrow meadowy bottom. The very Wye and its banks! winding in the moſt picturable manner ; with here and there a rugged rock riſing above the coppice wood ; its limits, with reſpect to this farm, cloſing, in a narrow ſecluded part, with a ſalmon weir, thrown acroſs the river ; forming a cataract of no mean effect. The lower part of the Valley is more open ; the river terminating, within ſight from the lovely ſwelling grounds of this *monaſtic demeſne*, in a winding eſtuary ;

ary; which is there margined with steep banks,—feathered to the water, with the woods of Mariftowe.

3.

JULY 15. Rode into CORNWALL; by Dinham Bridge, Beer-alfton, Calftock Paffage (Ferry), Calftock Church—New Bridge—acrofs the Heath—and back by Dinham Bridge.

A moft *romantic* ride! How much the fcenery of this Diftrict refembles that of Monmouthfhire, &c.: fteep wooded banks of rivers; here broken and rugged, there fhowing a fteeper face of rock. The heaths, on the Cornifh fide of the Tamer, ftrewed with blocks and fragments of granite, add to the favagenefs of the fcenery, whether viewed at hand or in diftance. And the inhabitants appear as rude and uncultivated as their Country: the Ferryman

at

3.

DISTRICT.

at Calftock is in the loweft ftage of civilization.

The Valley of the Tavey, at the height here croffed, is a mere dingle, wooded down to the river. But that of the Tamer, oppofite and below Calftock, is open, well foiled, and fet with orchards; the river, here, beginning to expand into an eftuary; the tide flowing fome mile or two above the Village of Calftock. Neverthelefs, its windings are moft abrupt and ftriking; the antient manfion of Curteel marking one of its bends, in the happieft manner.

LIMEKILNS.

The upper part of the eftuary is fet with limekilns on either fide; for the ufe of the Country near and above them, the ftones and culm being brought up in maft veffels*. The cultivated country is, now, everywhere ftudded with lime heaps.

SALMON WEIR.

Immediately above the tide's way is a Salmon Weir; and, above this, the wild favage fcenery juft defcribed; in the midft

of

---

* Obferved two dinner kettles boiling on the top of one of thefe kilns. If the nature of the fuel requires that the fire fhould burn outwardly, this is a frugal practice. If not, it is an extravagant way of dreffing dinners.

of which, near Newbridge, is a copper **3.**
mine, now working.

In this part of the ride, at the foot of HORSES.
Hingftone, one of the higheft of the Weftern mountains, I obferved two Cornifh
mares and foals, the fmalleft I have feen;
the mares not more, I apprehend, than
eleven hands high.   Young cattle, and
even oxen, are feen on thefe heaths.   But
no fheep appeared in any part of this
morning's ftroll.

The climature, even of the Vallies, is CLIMATE.
later than that of Eaft Devonfhire. Wheats
are ftill green.   On the Upper lands much
grafs is yet unmown! but evidently receiving great injury by ftanding.

The produce is corn, grafs, heath, and PRODUCE.
wood ; the two latter covering, in this rude
broken ride, much the largeft proportion of
furface.

4.

July 16. Rode to the SKIRTS OF THE DARTMORE HILLS; over Roborough Down, to Mavey, Walkhamton, &c. *

Roborough Down, with the chain of rough Commons which reach from hence to near Plymouth, forming an oblong depreſſed ſwell, has every appearance of being a fragment of the Dartmore Mountain †; from which it is ſeparated by an irregular Valley, containing three or four townſhips of cultivated land. Some of this land is of

a very

---

* In company with Mr. STAPLETON of BUCK-LAND : a man to whoſe ſuperior intelligence I owe much: a man who, with fourſcore years of experience, poſſeſſes an activity of body and mind, which many men, of half his years, would be happy to enjoy.

† It has been obſerved, however, that the prevailing ſtone of theſe Downs is very different, in compoſition and texture, from the quartzoſe granite of Dartmore and the Corniſh Mountains; between which this ſwell is ſituated: affording an intereſting ſubject to the Geologiſt.

a very fuperior quality; one confiderable plot of it letting at forty or fifty fhillings an acre, in this bleak and humid climate, and in this remote fituation.

The more central parts of this Valley now contain fome fine crops of wheat, and much tolerable barley. But the foil grows weaker, and lefs productive, as the Hills of Dartmore are approached.

The Sheep on the fkirts of the hills are moftly polled; but fome individuals are horned: they are very uneven as to carcafe: fome of them, neverthelefs, are not in a bad form.

The Cattle, feen in this morning's ride, are everywhere clean, and moftly of good frame. Chiefly of a dark red color; a few of them with white Glocefterfhire fpines. The fize that of Glocefterfhire, and Weft Suffex.

The Plow Team is chiefly Oxen. Saw fix good ones in a Team, in light work; yet did not perform, even that, with due effect. One of the pairs, with a proper plow, in good hands, would make much better work.

It

It may be remarked, that the Hundred, or ſubdiviſicn of the County, which includes a conſiderable part of the Diſtrict of Weſt Devonſhire, takes its name, or is underſtood to have taken its name, from the Common which I croſſed and repaſſed, this morning; or from ſome Town or Village which gave name to the Common; and of which there are at preſent no traces *.

In this ſtroll, I croſſed repeatedly the ARTIFICIAL BROOK, which waters the Town

---

* This correſponds with the tradition of Eaſt Devon-ſhire. (See page 132.) It is probable, however, that the Down, at leaſt, received its name from an extraordinary pile of rock, or large ſtones, the remains of which ſtill form a ſtriking object, on the face of theſe wild lands: bearing ſome reſemblance to the Tors of the Mountains. In the provincial dialect of the Diſtrict, *Roo*, is ſtill commonly uſed for *rough*; and *Burrow* is the ordinary name of a *heap*, whether of earth or ſtones (a combination which is ſtill ſtrictly preſerved in pronunciation). Under this rough pile of rocks, which may, heretofore, have been more conſiderable than it is at preſent, the huts of the firſt ſettlers may have been raiſed; or Druidical Aſſemblies have been held.

The etymons of the names of HUNDREDS, or DIVI-SIONS OF COUNTIES, are moſt difficult; and the Anti-quary, at leaſt, is intereſted in their elucidation.

Town of Plymouth, and which is taken
out of a fmall river, in one of the Vallies
of Dartmore. It is a treafure, not only to
Plymouth, but to the long range of dry
uplands, through which it paffes. This
public good owes its valuable exiftence to
one of the Drake family: namely, the
Grandfather of the prefent Sir Francis
Drake. He not only furnifhed the water,
from his own manor, but alfo the plan;
and, in difficult cafes, directed the execution.

5.

JULY 27. Yefterday, rode to TAMER-
TON, on the Eaftern banks of the Tamer;
diverfifying the road through this extraordinary paffage of country.

The furface is broken in a moft remarkable manner. The Stroudwater hills of
Glocefterfhire are not more diverfified.

R 3 But

5.
DISTRICT.

But a ſtill more extraordinary feature, of this little Diſtrict is formed, by bays, creeks, and inlets, of the eſtuary of the Tamer, winding in among the wooded hillocks, in a manner which I have nowhere elſe obſerved, in this Iſland; but in perfect reſemblance of the ordinary ſcenery, of the more broken margins, of the Weſt India and Bahama Iſlands.

Neverthelefs, the ſoil, where the Vallies have any width, is of a good quality; and even the tops of ſome of the ſwells are good arable land: ſo that, notwithſtanding the Country, in ſome points of view, appeaгs to be covered with wood, from the quantity which hangs on its ſteeper acclivities, it contains a conſiderable proportion of culti‧ vated ſurface.

SURVEYING
A DISTRICT.

The Crops, and the Syſtem of Manage‐ment, are the ſame as thoſe which I have obſerved, in my former rides: ſo ſoon is the general outline of Management caught!

TAMERTON
FAIR.

A Fair held yeſterday, at the ſweetly ſequeſtered Village of Tamerton Foliot, gave me an opportunity of ſeeing ſomething more of the Liveſtock of the Diſtrict.

The

The Cattle—provincially " Bullocks"— were moftly of the Weft Devonfhire, &c. breed: namely, bred on the Eaft and Weft banks of the Tamer: they are in general clean, well framed, and not ill flefhed: but there were few in a fit ftate to be *handled*.

5.
CATTLE.

Half a fcore remarkably fine oxen, eight or nine years old, of a fize and form for anything which is required of oxen, ftood as fat bullocks, for the butcher; but were barely forward enough for oil cakes, or other forcing food. If *fattened*, they would weigh eighty or ninety ftones (of 14lb.) a bullock.

GRAZING.

Alfo two " Barnftaple heifers"—in a beautiful form, and as foft as moles, at two years old! and for this reafon they were brought, here, to be fold to the butcher. What an error in practice! an error, I underftand, which is prevalent through the Country: there are two on *this* Barton, I find, in the fame predicament. Thofe which are of a nature to fat at two years old, are *murdered!* thofe which will not, are kept to breed from!

CATTLE.

BREEDING.

R 4   A few

5.
CATTLE,

A few fhorthorned and polled cattle were fhown : different Gentlemen, it feems, having introduced them into this County. But they are fortunately difliked by the farmers; who prefer their own breed; and, prejudice apart, they have good reafon for their partiality; their own being a much more eligible breed for a thinfoiled Diftrict. Their great defect is in milk, and perhaps this defect may have induced the Gentlemen of the County to bring in the Holdernefs breed; and, if they are kept merely for the dairy, no mifchief may enfue.

SHEEP.

The Sheep were moftly mountaineers— provincially "Moor Sheep:" thin, fcraggy, illformed creatures.

FAIRS.

The Fairs of this Country begin about eight o'clock, and laft till about twelve.

6.

July 29. Hitherto, I have been look-ing round me, and afcertaining facts.

1. I have traverfed the Country, for a few miles on every fide, and have gained a general idea of its outline of management.

2. I have ftudied a map of this noble Farm; traced its outlines; and furveyed, repeatedly, every field and parcel of it.

3. I have afcertained its prefent produce, or ftate of occupancy, by analyfing, claffing, and reuniting its various parts: thus bring-ing into one view the exact quantity of

  Culturable lands,
  Orchard grounds,
  Planted groves,
  Natural woodlands,
  Hedges, lanes, &c. &c. &c.

4. I have tabled the SUCCESSION, or ftate of occupancy of each individual field in cultivation,—during the LAST FOUR YEARS.

5. In

5. In the margin of this table, I have noted the fpecies and quantity of MANURE which each field has received, during that period; the term of the miniftry of the prefent " Hine."

6. I have regiftered the ARRANGE-MENT, tabled the crops and fallows, of THE PRESENT YEAR; fo as to fhow, *firft*, the number, name, fize, and crop of each field; arranged according to their refpective numbers in the map, which correfpond with their natural fituation in the farm: *fecondly*, the fields, arranged agreeably to their refpective crops; thus coming at the aggregate quantity of each; and, *thirdly*, the totals of thefe aggregates, to prove the truth of the analyfis *.

7. A table of the LIVESTOCK, now on the farm,

8. The quantity of MANURE IN STORE.

9. The

* This method I ftruck out, during my practice in Surrey (fee MINUTES OF AGRICULTURE IN SURREY), and have invariably followed it, in the different parts of the Ifland, in which I have practifed.

9. The IMPLEMENTS, &c. at prefent in ufe.

10. The WORKPEOPLE now employed.

Until thefe particulars be afcertained, and fpread out before the eye, fo as to be referred to, in the moft extemporary. way, no man fhould prefume to give orders, or fuggeft improvements, in hufbandry. Nor, then, until he has confidered well

The genius of the Country ; and

The locality of the given farm, as to markets, water carriage, &c. &c. ; alfo

Its natural characteriftics, or fitnefs for corn or grafs, dairying or grazing, &c. &c. taken collectively as a farm ; as well as

The afpect, foil, fubfoil, and ftate of tillage, of its feveral parts.

But, having duly informed himfelf in thefe requifites ; and having affiduoufly caught, and preferved, the hints for improvement, which firft impreffions may have furnifhed him with, any man, having previoufly an adequate knowledge of the general fubject, both in theory and practice, may venture to begin, with cautious ftep, to enter upon its improvement: being how-

6.

PRELIMINA-
RIES OF
IMPROVE-
MENT.

however, even then, careful not to derange the eſtabliſhed machine of management; until one, which is preferable, be ready to replace it: beginning with its more glaring improprieties aŋd defeẟs, as they occur fairly in the courſe of management; at once, to ſavc unneceſſary expence, and to prevent unneceſſary alarm,

7.

TILLAGE.

JULY 29. The lands of this farm are evidently much out of tilth. The young leys are overrun with fern, and thoſe of three or four years old are bare of graſs. But no wonder; they have been moſtly leyed, I find, agreeably to the cuſtom of the Country, after three ſucceſſive crops of grain; for which not more than three or four plowings are uſually given!

PLOW.

Indeed, were more to be aſſigned them, the Plow of the Country would be inadequate to the taſk of cleaning them. It is
the

the worſt Swing Plow I have ſeen. The
beam ſhort and clumſy, and the body long
and illformed, without a riſe or wreſt, to
force open the furrow ; the mold-board
being ſet high above the keel or ſoal of the
Plow ; which operates, in looſe ground, as
the Kentiſh Turnwreſt Plow ; making a
mark only, not opening a furrow *.

A foul piece of ground, intended for
Wheat, but which I wiſh to cleanſe tho-
roughly, for Barley the enſuing Spring, by
way of making a beginning in the great
work of purgation, I ſaw tantalized by this
ineffective implement.

However, by fixing a wreſt in the uſual
place, below the mold-board (the work of
a few minutes), it cleared its way, and
effected more in going once over the ground,
than the ſame Implement, without this
ſimple addition, would have done in going
over

---

* The DEVONSHIRE PLOW reſembles much, in general appearance, the Plow of the Herald and the Sign
Painter : a circumſtantial evidence, that it has heretofore
been prevalent in the Kingdom ; or that the Heraldic
Figures of this Country, and the Plow of Devonſhire, are
equally of Norman extraction.

over it almoſt any number of times; and this without vexing the Plowman, or alarming the Country, with "a new-faſhioned Plow."

Being deſirous, however, to get the Implement into a better form, and to adapt it to two Oxen or two Horſes, I have embraced an incident, to gain a pretence for conſtructing a Plow, ſuitable to that purpoſe. A ſmall plot of ground, which is ſo much encumbered with trees, that a team cannot work in it, and which has in conſequence been "hand beaten" and "hacked over," to free it from the foul ſtate in which it has long lain, was neverthelefs capable of being plowed, with a ſmall Plow, and a ſingle Horſe.

In conſtructing this little Implement, I ſuffered the Plow-wright to purſue his own beaten track, with reſpect to principal pieces and general conſtruction; deviating chiefly in the proportion of the ſeveral parts; making the beam proportionally longer and the body of the Plow ſhorter, than in the Plow of the Country: adding, however, a wreſt, and endeavouring to give the

mold-

mold-board the proper caſt. It fully anſwers the intended purpoſe; and bids fair to ſuperſede the introduction of the Yorkſhire Plow, for two Oxen or Horſes. It has, indeed, one main advantage over any alien Plow: it is ſet to work and regulated, as the ordinary Plow of the Country; is indeed a Devonſhire Sewl; and as ſuch it is held.

Seeing this, it ſtrikes me, that a ſimilar kind of ſucceſs may be obtained, in any Diſtrict, by adopting the general conſtruction of the faſhionable Plow of the Country, whether it be the Wheel, the Foot, or the Swing Plow; only altering the proportions, and giving the OPERATIVE PARTS the requiſite caſt.

June, 1795. Men, who have never attempted to introduce improvements in Agriculture, may conſider theſe ſacrifices, to the prejudices of eſtabliſhed cuſtoms, unneceſſary and trifling; but thoſe who have had experience, in this nice matter, will ſee their propriety.

JULY

8.

July 31. The Salmon fishery of the Tavey is appendant to this eftate. The Weir, which has been mentioned, is a work of confiderable magnitude and expence. It confifts of a ftrong dam or breaftwork, ten or twelve feet high, thrown acrofs the river, in a part where two projecting rocks ferve happily as buttreffes to the mafonry; which is built fomewhat compaffing or archwife (but not regularly nor fufficiently), to refift the preffure and force of the waters, in times of flood; when they are collected, by the flopes of the Dartmore Hills, and fent down with extraordinary impetuofity. At one end of the dam, is a " weir houfe" or TRAP; on the principle of the Vermin trap, whofe entrance is outwardly large; but contracted inwardly, fo as to elude or prevent the efcape of the animal which has taken it. It is

remarkable,

remarkable, however, with refpect to falmon, that although the entrance is by no means fo narrow as to prevent even the largeft from returning, it is believed that there is no inftance of thofe which have once entered, quitting their confinement, though they may have remained in it feveral days. A circumftance, perhaps, which can only be accounted for, in the natural propenfity, or inftinct, which directs them againft the ftream, and will not fuffer them to give up any advantage which they may have gained; the afcent into the trap being an effort of difficulty: in this cafe perhaps too great.

On the higher fide of the trap (which is fome twelve or fifteen feet fquare on the infide), oppofite to the entrance, is an opening or fluice in the ftone work,—or rather the rock,—as a paffage for the water. This opening has two lifting floodgates: the one clofe, to fhut out, occafionally, the whole of the water; the other a grate, to fuffer the water to pafs, and at tne fame time to prevent fifh of any confiderable fize from efcaping. When the trap is fet, the

VOL. II.   S   clofe

clofe gate is drawn up, with an iron crow: thus fuffering the water to pafs through the houfe. On the contrary, to take the fifh which have entered, the clofe gate is let down, and the trap is prefently left in a manner dry.

It is obfervable, that the narrowed entrance of the trap is judicioufly placed, fomewhat above the floor; fo that before the falmon are ferioufly alarmed by the fall of the water, it has funk below the mouth of the trap, and their retreat the more effectually cut off; for by following the water, near the floor, they are led away beneath the tunnel: which, like the open floodgate, &c. is made of ftrong wooden bars, open enough to permit the paffage of the water, but not that of the fifh.

The top or covering of the trap is a floor of planks, nearly level with the top of the weir; on the lower fide of which the trap is, of courfe, fituated.

Some days ago, when the water was unufually low—provincially and not improperly " fmall" — the whole river paffed through the weir houfe. But the recent

rains have fwoln it to a tenfold fize. The
water now pours over the weir, in a denfe,
broad fheet; fmooth, and glaffy above;
but furrowing as it defcends; and producing,
in its fall, a white foaming whirlpool;
the regularity of the fall being broken, on
one fide, by the torrent, rufhing down the
fteep defcent from the fluice, and, on the
other, by the margin of the river burfting
its way over the native rock,—a pleafing
object is produced; while the extreme
reclufenefs of the fituation, — the wild
coppice wood on the one hand, and the
high grown, impending timber on the other,
—add to the picturable effect of the fcene :
which, in a mild evening after rain, is ftill
heightened, and rendered more interefting,
by the animating and beautiful accompaniment of falmon, difplaying fetes of futile
agility;----throwing themfelves far out of
the water, in endeavouring to furmount the
cataract; or ftruggling, with more fatal
zeal, to reach the treacherous hold, from
whence there is no return.

The fpecies of fifh taken at this weir
are falmon, falmon peel — provincially

8.

SALMON
WEIR.

RIVER FISH.

"pail,"

8.

" pail," and, at fome certain feafons, a few trouts.

But the principal part of the produce of this fifhery is taken by NET FISHING. The river, for near a mile below the weir, is broken into rapids and pools, fome of them very deep. Seven or eight of thefe pools are adapted to the feine or draw net, which is drawn once, or twice a day, by four men: with horfes to carry the net, and the fifh caught; and with dogs to convey the end of the rope acrofs the water, where it is too deep or inconvenient to be forded.

The fifhing feafon commences, in *this* river (the Tavey), the middle or latter end of February (but 'on the Tamer not until feveral weeks afterward!), and clofes in October or November; when the weir is thrown open, and the fifh, afterward, fuffered to go up to fpawn.

Prefently after a flood, and when falmon are abundant, ten or twelve are frequently taken at a draught; fometimes more; upwards of a hundred, it is faid, were once drawn to fhore.

No

No wonder that a fishery thus productive, and lying at a distance from any habitation, should be liable to the depredations of POACHERS: especially as the river forms the boundary of a mining parish, notorious for its pilferers. They have been known to come down in bodies, like the game poachers of Norfolk; bidding ten or a dozen men defiance.

The net poaching is done, chiefly, in the night; while the river abounds with fresh water. But, in the day time, when the water is dead and clear, the poachers are not inactive; then using the spear, which they throw with dexterity; and, by this practice, are known to carry off numbers.

Nor does daylight deter them, wholly, from net fishing, when the water is favorable and fish in plenty. Yesterday, in passing, with the Hine and his son, through the meadows which margin the river, a party of three or four net poachers were discovered. They fled, on our approach; taking refuge among the underwood of the opposite banks; leaving behind them a net which has doubtless cost them the profits of many a month's illicit practice.

S 3 AUGUST

9.

August 1. The RAINS of this Country take a fingular appearance : at leaft, have done fo, in the commencement of the heavy fhowers, which have followed each other with little intermiffion, during feveral days paft. They come on, in a fort of mift, or fine rain : not of uniform denfity ; but driving before the wind, in perpendicular laminæ, with void interfpaces ; refembling more, in their proportions and general appearance, combs of honey in the hive, than any other object I can bring to my mind.

Thefe rains are brought by the Southweft wind ; are the produce of clouds arriving from the fea, and, being laid hold of by the high lands of this Diftrict, are checked in their courfe, and overtaken by thofe which follow ; thus becoming more and more denfe, until the heavieft rain is brought on.

On this theory, which is verified by fact, Cornwall and this Weftern and inter-

mountainous

mountainous Diftrict of Devonfhire, receive more rain than the Vale of Exeter; and this a greater quantity, than the more central Diftricts of the Ifland.

I have repeatedly obferved the high lands of Maker and Mountedgecumbe, which rife full to the view, from the higher grounds of this demefne, arrefting a cloud on its arrival from the channel; appearing to hold faft its lower limb, while the upper parts feemed eagerly haftening to the Dartmore Mountains; and while the furrounding Country was enjoying the fineft weather.

The fingular appearance, remarked above, may perhaps be accounted for, in its being the firft ftage of precipitation of the vapors which previoufly formed the unbroken cloud, or uniform mift. The vertical pofition of the laminæ apart, the appearance very much refembles that of the firft breaking of the cloud, produced by folutions of calcareous matter and fixed alkali; into the flocks which form, and follow each other to the bottom of the flafk.

S 4   AUGUST

10.

DISTRICT.   August 3. Rode to the VIRTUOUS
LADY; a mine, fituated on the banks of
the Tavey, a few miles northward of this
place, amidft the wildeft fcenery which
fteep-fided vallies, rocks, woods, and bleak
heaths, can well give.

ORCHARDS.   Not one new or interefting idea, in the
Rural Economy of Weft Devonfhire, ftruck
me, in this ftroll; except that of paring
off and fubverting, apparently with a Breaft
Plow, the "fpine" or rough fod of an orchard: not with a view of burning it; but
for the purpofe of letting it rot, as a "dreffing" or manure to the roots of the trees!
a practice, I underftand, which is not un-
ufual.   In this cafe, the orchard is rocky;
many ftones, or points of rock, appearing
above the furface.

Inverting the fward may not operate
more as a manure, than as, by checking the
vegetation of the grafs and weeds, it may

give

give additional air, moifture, and freedom
to the fibrils of the roots of the fruit trees.

Nothing, indeed, could well effect this
purpofe better. For the inverted turf being
laid flat, and evenly over the furface, the
fhoots from the roots which are not deftroyed by the cutting, may be fmothered,
or checked, by the covering.

II.

AUGUST 7. I have, at length, got a
WHIP-REIN PLOW fully into its work, in
the field. See MIN. 7.

The firft day, the horfes were led. The
fecond driven, with reins; by a youth,
walking at the fide of the plow; as much
to make the horfes tractable, and render the
new operation lefs irkfome to the plowman,
as to teach the young man the ufe of the
reins, in harrowing; which is here two
perfons work; even though but one horfe
were employed.

This,

11.
PLOWING.

This, the third day, the horſes are become tractable; and the plowman is guiding
and driving them himſelf: making, with
two ſorry rips, and the light plow above
deſcribed, as good work, as ſix oxen are
making, in the ſame field, and the ſame
work, with the clumſy tool of the Country.

INTRODU-
CING
WHIP REINS.

IN FUTURE,—let two plowmen aſſiſt in
the introduction of whip reins, holding and
driving alternately: thus, while the horſes
are rendered manageable, the plowmen will
learn the uſe of the reins.

12.

COPPICE
HEDGES.

AUGUST 8. A great defect and incon-
veniency of the MOUND COPPICE FENCES
of this Diſtrict, I ſee, is their being liable
to be torn down by ſtock, whether cattle
or ſheep, ſcraping away the baſe of the
mound, and letting down the ſides, perhaps
in wide ſhoots. The ſoil thus ſhot down
is a ſtep to greater miſchief; and, if not
ſtopt, a paſſage is made, acroſs the mound.

To

To prevent thefe mifchiefs, many
" hedges" of the Diftrict, and particularly
of this eftate, have been faced with ftone :—
the ordinary flate rock of the country ;
moftly fet on-edge, or rather on-end ; which,
by the people of the Country, is confidered
as preferable to laying them horizontally,
in the mafon's manner. Moft of the fences
of this farm have been faced with ftone, on
both fides ; at an expence, from firft to laft,
equal perhaps to the fee fimple value of
the land. For, as the roots in the body of
the mound fwell, the facing is of courfe
bulged out, and is at length thrown down ;
thus leaving the fence, if not timely re-
paired, in a worfe ftate than thofe which
have been left free for blackthorns, and
other brufhwood, to grow and defend the
fides of the banks.

Where this brufhwood has got hold, and
outlived the overhanging, and drip, of
widefpreading coppice wood, growing on
the top of the mound, the fides are fecure ;
for being cropped and ftunted by pafturing ftock, they have grown, in many
parts, thick and impervious : and it is extraordinary,

traordinary, that the idea of planting or encouraging fuch brufhwood, and ftriking off the overhanging topwood, to prevent its being checked in its growth, fhould not have taken place ; inftead of that of facing the fides with ftones ; fetcht, perhaps, fome diftance on horfeback.

Seeing the evident propriety of this treatment, I have been applying it to a hedge, of three or four years growth, from the laft cutting ; as a fpecimen, or pattern, for the remainder of fuch as will admit of its application.

The blackthorns and other fhrubs, which grow at the foot of the mound, and on its fides, I have endeavoured to fpread, over the face of the mound ; faftening them, there, with hooked pins, as fruit trees to a wall : firft clearing the brambles and weeds which grew before and behind them ; and, afterward, trimming off the loofe fpray on the face of the whole : whether thorn, furze, bramble, or briar. Finally, with a long handled hook, ftriking off the over-hanging boughs of the coppice wood ; leaving a regular face, as even as the live ftuff, ſtuff, at preſent, will admit of : not perpendicular; but leaning ſomewhat inward, towards the middle of the fence ; ſo as to give every twig, from the bottom to the top, light, air, and headroom.

An advantage of this operation, beſide that of putting the fence in the way of improvement, is that of freeing the borders from weeds and brambles, and from the drip and ſhade of outhanging boughs.

13.

AUGUST II. Rode to the head of "PLYMOUTH LEAT."*

This ARTIFICIAL BROOK is taken out of the river MEW, towards its ſource ; at the foot of Sheepſtor Tor ; in a wild mountain dell.

I expected

* *Leat, Late,* or *Lake,* as it is ſometimes pronounced, is perhaps a corruption of *Lead* or Conductor ; being applied, I believe, to any artificial channel for conducting water.

13.

PLYMOUTH
BROOK.

I expected to have found an accurate gauge, to regulate the quantity of water; agreeably to the act of parliament, under which it is taken. But in this I was difappointed. The Mew, itfelf, is there but a moderately fized brook. Acrofs it a weir or dam is formed, of large rough ftones, with which the bed of the brook is thickly ftrewed. A paltry, ill fhapen, wooden frame or floodgate, with a gully underneath it (through which moft of the water paffes), receives about half the waters of the Mew; now lower than ufual, but not at their loweft. In the dam is another floodgate; lying lower than that of the made brook, to draw off the water from this, during repairs.

The channel of the Leat differs, in dimenfions, according to the ground it is led over. Acrofs open plain ground, it is ten or twelve feet wide, with flat floping banks; the water running fix or eight inches deep, according to the defcent; which is generally fufficient to make it ripple gently over the pebbles, with which its bottom is ftrewed; forming a living ftream, a lovely brook.

The

The chief difficulty, in executing this valuable work, was in carrying it round the point of an almoft perpendicular rock; where a wooden aqueduct was firft corftructed; but where a more fubftantial Channel has fince been formed, with mafonry.

It is obfervable that the mill of Mavey, fituated beneath this brook, and fed by the fame fource, the Mew,—and about whofe waters, for want of accurate and fubftantial regulators, a perpetual contention is kept up,---is fed by an artificial channel, perfectly refembling the Leat under defcription. The mill of Milton, near this place, is fupplied with water, in a fimilar manner. And, it is highly probable, thefe Mill Leats furnifhed the defigner with the idea of the Plymouth Brook *.

Whatever fortunate thought gave rife to it, its utility is great: not only in fupplying a populous town with water; but in

watering

13.
PLYMOUTH
BROOK.

MILL LEATS.

MADE
BROOKS.

---

* In fome part of the Mill Leat of Mavey, a ftone, I was told, is placed, with the date, 1600, upon it. The artificial Brook, or New River, of London was executed about 1610.

watering a chain of uplands, fifteen or twenty miles in extent. The gratification experienced in falling in, abruptly, as frequently happens, with fo ample a ftream, in places where fuch an object is the leaft expected, yet where it is moft wanted, is of a fingular and fuperior kind.

How many fituations, in this Ifland, wanting fuch relief, might have it in a fimilar way.

Where a fufficient quantity of water ean be had at the fource, much of the coft might be repaid, by letting off branches; to the adjacent country.

Upon Roborough Down, a rill is taken out of the Plymouth Brook, for the ufe of a Gentleman, who lives fome two miles off, clofe by the banks of the Tamer! This rill not only fupplies his houfe, but furnifhes water to pafturing ftock, in its way.

In this cafe, the quantity of water is accurately regulated, by a perforated ftone, fet on edge, in a fort of ftone trough ; the aperture circular, and about three and a half inches diameter : furnifhing a fufficient

fupply,

supply, if frugally managed, for a hamlet or village.

But the ancient rights of WATER MILLS are bars to improvements of this nature, as well as to the watering of lands : rights, however, which might, *now*, be alienated without exceffive inconvenience to the community ; windmills and fteam engines rendering them no longer *necesfary*; though, in fome fituations, a few might ftill be ufeful.

14.

AUGUST 12. Rode to PLYMPTON, in the SOUTH HAMS of Devonfhire.

The fcenery about Plymbridge is fweetly reclufe ; forming a happy contraft to the open view from Lord Boringdon's arches ; from whence Plymouth Sound and Harbour, with the interefting fcenery which furrounds them, are feen immediately under the eye.

VOL. II.   T   A broad

14.

DISTRICT.

A broad view of the South Hams is alſo commanded from this proud point.

The Country immediately below it, about Ridgeway and the Plymptons, is ſingularly broken ; yet moſt of it well ſoiled.

PLYMPTON
FAIR.

A Fair, of ſome repute, led me to Plympton, this morning.   But it fell ſhort of my expectation.   About a hundred and fifty head of cattle, chiefly cows and calves ; with a few half-fat oxen, and leſs than half-fat cows.   Alſo a few pens of ſheep ; moſtly poor thin-carcaſed animals. Altogether a mean collection.

PLYMPTON.

The Borough of Plympton is moſt enviably ſituated.   The climature mild, almoſt, as that of the South of Europe. The ſcenery around it delightful ; and the ſoil of a ſuperior quality ; yet, in its nature, dry and clean. . Proviſions of every kind abundant and cheap.   The Town, or rather large genteel Village, is itſelf neat ; its inhabitants reſpectable ; and it is ſituated near a great public road, without being incommoded by it.

AUGUST

15.

AUGUST 12. (See MIN. 12.) Some older hedges, on the fides of harveft roads, whofe boughs were grown too large, and reached too high, to be cut from the ground, I have had " pared" in the following manner.

Put two oxen to a waggon, and two men into it, with hooks of different lengths; placing the waggon clofe to the hedgebank. In this fituation, the men were level with their work; cutting out the larger boughs, with common hedge bills, and ftriking off the fpray, with lighter tools; the waggon proceeding with the work.

In this way, the two men cleared, in the courfe of yefterday afternoon, not lefs than a hundred rods, fufficiently to prevent the corn from being thrafhed out, or torn off the harveft waggons, by the outhanging

T 2   boughs.

15.

TRAINING
HEDGES.

boughs. A difpatch which could not have
been obtained in any other manner.

Even in the training of younger hedges
(of this Country), a waggon might be employed with advantage.

16.

RECLAIM-
ING LAND.

August 13. Clearing arable
lands from stones. The foils of this
Diſtrict are much incommoded with ſtones
of different kinds; but chiefly with the
ſlate rock, of which the Country may be
ſaid to be formed; and a ſpecies of chryſtal
—provincially "whitaker"—which is frequently met with in large blocks, either
entire, or partially incorporated with the
ſlate rock.

A field, now under fallow,—which has
long been noted for ſewl-breaking, I am
clearing in this way. The plowman carries,
in the body of his ſewl, a parcel of ſmall
rods; and, where he finds a ſtone, ſets up
one

one of his marking ſticks. Two men follow, with ſhovels, mattocks, and crows,
raiſing the *ſtones*; and baring the *rocks*, to
be raiſed, at leiſure, by men accuſtomed to
quarry work. Thus, at a comparatively
trifling expence, the land is freed, plow-
furrow deep, for ever, from obſtructions:
not only of the plow, but of harrows;
which would now be ſeen riding upon flat
ſtones, from one end of the field to the
other, were not a perſon employed to follow,
and releaſe them from ſo aukward and unprofitable a ſituation: leaving, however,
the ſtones upon the land; left this part of
his employment ſhould be wanting, in future.

I 7.

August 27. Clearing foul lands.
(See Min. 7.) This and another piece,
ſtill fouler, and in a worſe ſtate of tillage, I
have treated, and intend to treat, in the
following manner.

About a month ago, one of theſe fields,
then in a ſtate of looſe broken ground, was

laid

17.

RECLAIM-
ING LAND.

laid up into narrow ribs (the gardener's trenches) by a half plowing; with a wrefted plow, and with the ftern fet TEN INCHES wide; forcing up the ridgets, as high and fharp as poffible; in order to deftroy the root weeds, by drought, and by breaking their field of pafturage; and to give the feeds of weeds an addition of air and furface to promote their vegetation.

About a week ago, the firft-plowed part was harrowed acrofs the ribs, with long-tined harrows;—levelling the furface completely, and following them with a roller and finer harrows, hung behind it: thus grinding down every clod, and effectually deftroying every feedling weed which had vegetated.

TILLAGE.

The furface is now thickly fet with another crop of feedling weeds,—which I am turning under by ONE DEEP PLOWING, acrofs the former ribs, and in narrow plits, but with a BROAD SHARE, and with a STERN TWELVE INCHES WIDE; thus moving every particle of the foil, about TEN INCHES DEEP (fome inches deeper, perhaps, than it has ever been plowed before)

before), leaving the furface rough and cloddy.

17.

Over this rough furface, I am fpreading a moderate dreffing of yard dung; to be dragged and rolled and harrowed, until the dung be effectually incorporated, with the frefh raw foil, brought up; thereby to meliorate it, and to *force* the feeds of weeds, with which it has, no doubt, been amply fupplied, century after century.

MANURING.

The weed feeds having fpent themfelves, and the crude foil having received the influence of the atmofphere, the dreffing will be turned in, with a mean-depth or fomewhat fhallow plowing; and the furface be fuffered to remain in the rough ftate, in which the plow leaves it, during winter.

FALLOWING.

In the fpring, as foon as the clods have thrown out their feedling weeds, and the weather will permit, the furface will be ground down to powder, to provoke the remainder to vegetation; and, in due feafon, be fown with barley and ley herbage.

Thus, for the lofs of ONE YEAR'S RENT, thefe fields will probably be benefited for twenty years to come.

The

1794. The fuccefs has anfwered the fulleft expectation. The field which was managed more immediately under my own eye, is, I am of opinion, five pounds an acre better for the operation; reckoning on twenty years, from the time of performing it.

It is obfervable, that, in every cafe where circumftances will allow it, an EIGHTEEN MONTHS FALLOW fhould be broken up, in autumn, or early winter, by a rib plowing; fuffering it to lie, in an expofed ftate, during winter. This, befides employing the winter's frofts in the great work of purification, forwards the bufinefs of the enfuing fummer, and renders the whole operation a matter of leifure and conveniency; and, in the end, COMPLEAT: putting the foil in its moft profitable ftate of exertion, for a length of years. Under proper management and with the affiftance of FALLOW CROPS, Lands, THUS EFFECTUALLY RECLAIMED, may not require a repetition of the operation, for half a century afterwards.

18.

AUGUST 28. A field of twenty-four acres was fowing with Turneps, when I arrived here;—with too little tillage, too little feed, and fome of it with dung much too long; the harrows drawing the feed into ftripes and bunches. The confe-quence is, the crop is irregular, and the few plants which appear are nearly fuffo-cated in wild Muftard, and other weeds.

Some light hoes were ordered to be made, from old fithe blades; and fix of them were put into the hands of women, who had never hoed, and one into the hands of a man, who had.

The directions, in going the firft time over the ground, were, to thin the clufters or bunches, and to check the weeds; without attempting to fet the Turnep plants out, fingly, or at full diftances; and even, in doing this, to proceed flowly at the outfet.

Hitherto,

18.

Hitherto, they have performed this work better than was expected. Indeed, by adhering to the rules, here laid down, Turnep hoers will ſpontaneouſly grow out of them. By ſetting off ſlowly, and not attempting too great nicety, at firſt, the employment becomes pleaſurable, and the eye and the hands are imperceptibly taught the art: eſpecially if the greater errors which ariſe be, from time to time, pointed out, by one who is converſant in the operation.

They have now begun to go over the firſt-ſown part, a ſecond time; ſetting out the plants ſingly, and at due diſtances; namely ten to twelve inches apart (the hoes being eight inches long); except where two plants ſtand near each other, in a vacant ſpace; in which caſe, both plants are permitted to ſtand *.

Hoing Turneps, with eight inch hoes, made from ſithe blades, is moderate work for women (ſuch hoes are light and paſs freely

* For more particular remarks and directions, reſpecting this operation, ſee Mid. Econ. Vol. II. P. 198.

freely through the foil) ; and, by proceeding on the principles here adopted, any
woman, with an eye and hands, may be
foon taught the art: will, in one full
feafon, become a fufficient Turnep hoer.

How eligible, in Countries where women
are not employed in reaping, to teach them
the ufe of the Turnep hoe. What avails
the flownefs of their work, the firft feafon,
compared with the introduction of fo valuable a practice : efpecially to a large occu-
pier ; and, ftill more, to a man of large
eftate.

19.

SEPTEMBER I. It is cuftomary, here,
to fhoe working oxen ; although they are
rarely employed upon the road. The
ftoninefs of the foils, and rockinefs of the
lanes and driftways, may account for the
practice.

In the form of the fhoes, or the method
of fetting them on, I fee little new. A few
parti

particulars of practice, neverthelefs, require
to be noticed. Having been caft, or thrown,
and his legs bound together, in the ufual
manner, the animal is forced nearly upon
his back, and his feet hoifted up to a convenient height, by means of a forked pole,
fome five feet long; the fork taking the
bandage which birds the feet, the other
end being fixed firmly in the fward, upon
which they are ufually thrown. This
fimple contrivance gives great firmnefs,
fteadinefs, and conveniency to the operation..

That the individuals may be the more
conveniently laid hold of, and trammelled,
the team are driven to the place of fhoeing,
in their yokes, and hung together with
chains, the hindmoft chain being faftened
to a large root, or ftool, in the hedge; by
the fide of which they are ufually placed;
in order to prevent their running off, on
feeing one of their companions thrown
down and roughly treated, in their fight,
—immediately under their eyes!

Today, the remaining three of a team,
fhoeing in this extraordinary way, being
alarmed

alarmed and rendered favage, by feeing the favage treatment of their comrades, broke from their hold; ran off; the pair throwing down the fingle ox encumbered by his yoke;—dragged him;—broke off one of his horns, with its core clofe to his head; cut the finew of his fore leg, almoft through, with one of the hooks; and have thus *entirely fpoilt him*.

Some means of facilitating the fhoeing of oxen are much to be defired. I am of opinion that were rearing calves, which are intended for work, accuftomed to have their feet taken up, and their hoofs beaten with a hammer; and were a repetition of this practice to take place, in the winter feafon, when the fteers are in the yards, or in ftalls, they might afterwards be fhod as horfes.

Working cattle fhould alfo be accuftomed, from their earlieft age, to be driven and led about, fingly; fhould be wholly reclaimed from a ftate of wildnefs; as working horfes are.

The ox, under kind and generous treatment, is eafily familiarized, and rendered docile.

20.

LONDON, 1794. Having, in the fummer of 1790, fpent fome months at Maidftone; in Kent; to regifter the HOP CULTURE, and the other branches of Rural Economy, as they are practifed in that fertile Diftrict; and having, in the Spring and early part of the Summer of 1791, paid fome attention to the Farnham practice of cultivating hops, as well as to that and other Rural Subjects, in Weft Suffex; I judged it expedient to return to Farnham, early in September, in the fame year, to be prefent at the picking and curing, in that Diftrict; in order to enable me, the better, to draw up a practical account of the management of the Hop; in a general account of the Rural Practice of the SOUTHERN COUNTIES; which I hope foon to offer to the Public.

Before I left Buckland, I digefted the ideas which I had collected, refpecting the prefent

prefent ftate and improvement of its charming demefne. Many of thofe ideas related, of courfe, to private concerns; many of them appear, in the foregoing Digeft, of the practice of the Diftrict at large; and others, in the preceding Minutes. Some few of them, however, have not yet been introduced into this Work; and thefe are inferted, here. For what applies to the Barton of Buckland is more or lefs applicable to the lands of the furrounding Country, and may furnifh hints for thofe of other Diftricts.

20.

IMPROVE-
MENTS
SUGGESTED.

This, in foil and furface, is properly a SHEEP FARM. Sheep, Turneps, Barley, temporary Leys, and Wheat, ought certainly to be confidered as PRIMARY OBJECTS. The DAIRY feems to ftand fecond; as being, in this fituation, profitable in itfelf; and as a fource of working cattle. But no part of it appears to be well adapted to the GRAZING OF CATTLE,

OBJECTS OF
HUSBAN-
DRY.

TLE, which prefents itfelf as a fubordinate object; to be confined merely to the aged cows and oxen, which the farm itfelf throws off. A main object, on many accounts, is to keep the manager at home. Hence, adopt a courfe of tillage, fuitable to the foil and fituation; with liveftock fuitable, in fpecies and proportion, to the crops: adhering as clofely to this outline of management, as feafons and circum- ftances will permit. Under thefe regu- lations, the Hine would have little to take off his attention from the interior operations of the farm; except the difpofal of its immediate produce. He would have no riding about the Country to buy ftock, nor any trifling away of his time, in felling them.

Farming and jobbing can feldom be united, with profit: even by a Principal; much lefs by an Agent.

Some RIVER BREAKS are wanted to defend the meadow lands. Stones, not timber, appear to be the proper materials for thefe Breaks.

1794.

1794. Hitherto, piles and planks had been ufed, to confine the rapid Tavey within its channel; much valuable timber having been ufed, from time to time, in " weiring;" while the bed of the river is ftrewed with ftones, fit for this purpofe.

I had one conftructed, as a fpecimen, in the moft difficult fituation;—immediately in front of the Salmon Weir, and within the reach of its whirlpool, in times of floods; at one fourth of the expence which a timber break would have coft. It is built with *dry ftones*, collected from the river bed.

The permanency of this loofe ftonework depends, entirely, on the *principle of con-ftruction*. The face of the Break is every way bulging towards the force of the current; which acts upon it, as fuper-incumbent weight on an arch. The bafe line, fome fifteen or twenty yards long, is the fegment of a circle, with its outer or convex fide to the water. The wall, from four or five, to two or three feet high, is carried up *battering*, very confiderably, from the ftream; not with a ftraight line,

VOL. II.   U   but

but fomewhat convex, and rounding off at the top,—until it forms nearly a horizontal paving. The ftones are laid, with their larger ends inward; and not horizontally, but dipping, in fuch a manner, as to lie fquare with the face of the wall; which is thus placed in the pofture of *falling*, towards the bank of earth, that was rammed in firmly behind, as the wall was carried up. The whole to be filled in, level with the adjoining meadow; thick turf being firmly laid, in continuation of the pavement; that the water, when it overflows the meadow, may pafs fmoothly over the break, and thereby prevent the adjoining fward from being torn up, by a difturbed current.

A violent flood difplaced fome of the uppermoft ftones, for want of the ground being filled up, and properly finifhed, behind them; and the eddy of the Weir pool fcooped away part of the gravel from the foundation, fo as to endanger it; until large ftones were thrown againft it, for its defence.

Where there is a proper choice of ftones;
and

and if the top and foundation be from time to time attended to; a river Break, built on thefe principles, may endure for a length of years.

The prefent dairy cows, fome few excepted, accord ill with the Barton of Buckland: which is entitled, in every point of view, to the fineft breeds of liveftock the Ifland at prefent poffeffes. The degenerate breed, now upon it, are unprofitable, even as dairy ftock, and are altogether unfit, as molds for working oxen; the breeding of which ought to be a principal object in keeping them. Some of the oxen, the defcendants of the old ftock of the farm, are almoft unexceptionable : their fize being their principal deficiency. The prefent degeneracy of the cattle appears to have arifen out of a wrong principle of management, of the late hines; namely, that of felling everything inclined to fatnefs, fo as to fetch money; and buying in anything for cheapnefs, without regard to fpecific quality *.

U 2　　　　　　　The

* This error in practice has been mentioned before; but it is of fo treacherous and mifchievous a nature, it cannot be too often reprobated.

The Salmon Fifhery, at prefent, is a nurfery of Poachers; owing not fo much to the remotenefs of its fituation, with refpect to the houfe, as to the fkreens of wood, which now rife on either fide of the river; and hide them, in a great meafure, from detection. Under its prefent management, it is an object worth their attending to, and of courfe draws them off from honeft, but lefs profitable, employments. The moft eligible courfe to be taken appears to be that of throwing difficulties in their way; fo as to make it not worth their attention. To attempt to prevent them by force, efpecially while the mines remain open, would evidently be imprudent.

Perhaps, the men, who are employed in drawing the net, fhould be paid not by the tide, or the number of times they draw it, but by the number, or weight, of the fifh caught: thus uniting their own intereft with that of their employer. Even night fifhing might, by this means, be confiderably checked; not fo much by keeping watch, as by every pool being fifhed *carefully*, before the night came on. Now, if the net be wetted, their hire is due.

Or *perhaps* deftroy the net-fifhing altogether ; by placing obftructions in the
pools ; and depend folely on the Weir :
which, if properly regulated and duly attended, would perhaps receive all the fifh
which enters the river ; or, in much probability, a far greater number, than are now
legally taken, by the weir and nets jointly.
Giving a weir man a fixed proportion of the
produce,—for his attendance during the
fifhing feafon,—for feeing that the pools
were kept guarded to prevent net fifhing,—
for keeping down the fkreens, -- and for
attending daily and hourly, during dead
water, to prevent fpearing,—would, in this
cafe, be requifite.

At prefent, the Fifhery is either neglected, or it interferes, unprofitably, with
the ordinary bufinefs of the Farm.

On whatever principle a Fifhery of this
kind is conducted, the perfons employed in
it ought to be rewarded, in proportion to
the quantity taken ; efpecially when they
are not immediately under the eye of their
employer.

U 3   O<small>CTOBER</small>

21.

October 30. Rode to Milton Abbots; by Tavistock and Lamerton.

Some charming grafslands about Taviftock; ftill better before Lamerton; and yet more excellent, at Milton Abbots.

Confiderable herds of fine oxen, and good fatting cows, are now in thefe grounds: fome of which are ftill full of grafs;—highly colored, and apparently of a fuperior quality.

How extraordinary, that Plots, fuch as thefe are, fhould be fcattered in fo bleak and barren a Country. Between Lamerton and Milton, an unproductive Heath intervenes; the rich lands of the latter being nearly furrounded with fuch Heaths, and overlooked by Mountains: the fituation inhofpitable in the extreme. The fertile lands of Lamerton and Taviftock are infulated in a fimilar manner.

But

But the extent of thefe lands, collectively, is fmall: and in a furvey of the Rural
Practice of the Weft of England, they are
rather a fubject of admiration, than of importance,

22.

NOVEMBER 1. The ROUGHCAST
work of this Diftrict is executed in a fuperior manner; being not only durable, but
pleafing to the eye.

Some lately done at Ivybridge is equal,
in beauty, to dreffed ftone work. Mr. Stapleton's houfe, in this neighbourhood,
done in a fimilar way, has now ftood upwards of half a century; and, excepting at
the immediate foundation, and beneath
fome of the windows, where water has
been fuffered to lodge, the whole remains
as firm as when firft done; appearing to
have acquired a ftonelike texture. In both
thefe cafes Chryftaline gravel has been ufed;

U 4   and

and both of them are falſe-jointed, to re-
ſemble dreſſed ſtone work.

An intelligent workman, whom I acci-
dentally converſed with on this ſubjeƈt,
ſuggeſted an admirable *theory* of the
operation of roughcaſting ; making an
accurate diſtinƈtion between this and Stucco
work.

STUCCO being laid on, *in a ſtate of paſte*,
more or leſs air is unavoidably ſhut up,—
let it be ever ſo well worked ; and the very
expanſion and contraƈtion of this air, by
heat and froſt, is ſufficient to break the
texture of the Stucco. Beſide, let the
working be done ever ſo carefully, cracks,
though not evident to the eye, will be
formed in drying ; and if, by means of theſe
microſcopic fiſſures (or of thoſe formed by
the expanſion and partial eſcape of the confined air), water take poſſeſſion of the air
cells, the periſhing and peeling become natural conſequences.

ROUGHCAST, on the contrary, being
applied, *in a fluid ſtate*, and by little and
little, fills up every pore, and cranny in the
face of the wall ; as well as in the face of
every

every fucceeding coat; which being fuffered to dry, before another coat is added,
the cracks, if any take place, are filled up;
and *deep* ones, of courfe, are effectually prevented: whereas, the cracks of Stucco
neceffarily reach through the coat.

STUCCO evidently partakes of the nature
of cement ufed, in a ftate of pafte or mortar;
LIQUID COATING, of cement poured into
the wall, in a ftate of grout.

STUCCO is analogous to the materials of
a dam, or the bank of a canal, formed with
earth, in a ftate of pafte: ROUGH COAT-
ING, to the puddle of Canal Makers: to
loam intimately mixed with water, and
permitted to fubfide in a liquid ftate: thus
preventing air cells; and forming a clofe,
homogeneous mafs,

23.

DECEMBER 10. TURNEPS. (See MIN.
18.) Several acres of thefe Turneps were,
in my abfence, omitted to be hoed. I
found

found them, overgrown with Charlock,—a yard high, and as yellow as a Rape field: the feeds of the lower pods being fully formed. Part had been drawn by hand, according to the cuftom of the Country, and thrown in heaps: an expenfive and wafteful practice.

A few cart loads were ordered to be mown,—high enough to prevent, as much as poffible, the injury of the Turneps,—and low enough, to get beneath the pods of the Charlock; and were ftrewed over an adjoining pafture ground.

Sheep eat the tips of the leaves of the Turneps, partially cut off by the fithe; and alfo the leaves of the Charlock; but left the pods and the ftalks of the latter, in a great meafure untouched.

Cattle, however, preferred the Charlock; eating the whole up, clean; before they picked up the Turnep leaves.

Four or five acres kept about twenty head of young and ftore cattle, near three weeks. Had the food been given to them regularly, and more frugally than it was, it would have kept them, fufficiently as

ftore

ſtore cattle, a month. This, added to the ſaving of the expence, compared with that of drawing, cannot be reckoned at leſs than twenty ſhillings an acre.

They eat it ſo voraciouſly, that one or two of them were repeatedly blown, or ſufflated, by it : and a heifer failed ſo much, while at this food, that it was thought right to have her butchered. On opening her, however, her diſorder appeared evidently to have been of ſome duration; a part of her inteſtines being in a ſtate of decay. The pungency of the Charlock might, or might not, have ſtimulated her diſorder.

Be this as it may, it is ſufficiently proved, that healthy cattle may be kept on Charlock in pod, with ſafety and profit *.

DECEM-

* Part of it, the rough Charlock or WILD MUSTARD (*Sinapis Arvenſis*); part, the ſmooth Charlock, or WILD Rape (*Braſſica Napus*);

24.

DECEMBER 10. The only ufeful idea
I have been able to collect, from the late
manager of this farm, is his method of cutting garden Cabbages.

Inftead of clearing the ftalk or ftem from
the lower leaves, and crofs-flitting the
crown or top of the ftalk, in the ufual
manner,—he cuts out the body of the
Cabbage, only ; letting all the open, large,
fpreading leaves, remain upon the ftem.

The confequence is a fecond, and perhaps a third, crop of *Cabbages*; not one,
but many, upon a ftem ; forming, by the
third crop, a Cabbage tree. There are
now, in the garden of this place, feveral
ftems, with four, five, or more wellfized
table Cabbages on each : and, applied to
field Cabbages, which are cut early, the
principle may be a good one. The old
leaves continue to draw up the fap, until
vigorous

vigorous fhoots are formed; when they are obferved to droop, decay, and fall at the foot of the plant; being, perhaps, in every ftage of their decay, ufeful to the young progeny; in fhading the ground, in keeping down the weeds, and in furnifhing a fupply of mephitic gas to their rifing offspring: advantages which are loft, in the ordinary method of treatment. Many of the plants are killed by the fudden check of the fap, and thofe which furvive, throw out numerous, and of courfe, weak fhoots; few of them fwelling to any fize, or taking the Cabbage form.

25

DECEMBER 18. A SOCIETY of AGRICULTURE, I underftand, is now forming in the South Hams. In my late excurfion, through that Diftrict, I heard of a "Plowing Match," at Kingfbridge, and another, at Ivybridge; where Meetings of Country Gen-

Gentlemen, and fubftantial Yeomen, diftri-
buted REWARDS TO GOOD WORKMEN :
a rational Inftitution, which, while it continues to adhere to this principle, cannot
fail of proving beneficial to the Country.

If mere PRECEPTIVE SOCIETIES, without the power of EXAMPLE, IN THEM-
SELVES, can be materially ferviceable to the
advancement of Agriculture, their object,
I am of opinion, ought to be that of EN-
COURAGING GOOD HUSBANDRY, among
PROFESSIONAL MEN : of fearching for
SUPERIOR HUSBANDMEN ; and diftinguifhing them, in fuch manner, as to create
a fpirit of emulation ; and of affifting fuch
diftinguifhed Managers to procure the requifite means of improvement. Thus
placing them in a confpicuous light, and
making them the honorable inftruments
of that example, which a mere preceptive
Society has not, in itfelf, the power of
fetting.

But, on a LARGE ESTATE, this may be
the beft done, by its Proprietor. He
knows, or ought to know, the individuals
who are moft worthy of being made the
diftin-

distinguished leaders of its improvement: and, in this cafe, he can encourage them, according to their merit; without being liable to the cabals of Theorifts and Adventurers, to which mixed Societies are ever subject. A few pounds expended, annually, among his own tenants, in stimulating them to accurate management, would, in most cafes, pay him tenfold interest *.

These reflections suggest Institutions of a higher order. Let men of landed property affociate: not fo much for the particular purpofe of ENCOURAGING GOOD HUSBANDRY among their tenants, as for the more general intention of afcertaining the fuitable regulations, under which to conduct the MANAGEMENT of ESTATES.

For

* In a Sketch of the RURAL ECONOMY of the CENTRAL HIGHLANDS of Scotland, which I had the honor of prefenting, in 1794, to the BOARD of AGRICULTURE, as a Report concerning that part of the Ifland, I purfued this idea; propofing to divide a large eftate into Diftricts, or Officiaries; and to place a fuperior Manager in each, as a diftinguifhed Leader, in Rural Improvements.

25.

ASSOCIA-
TIONS OF
LANDED
GENTLE-
MEN.

For feeing, evidently, not only in the Diſtrict under ſurvey, but in other Diſtricts of the Iſland, that a greater defalcation of public and private property is incurred, through the inaccurate management of landed property, than through the errors of cultivation, it belongs excluſively to the poſſeſſors of eſtates to rectify the impropriety *.

The

* I am deſirous of being fully underſtood. There are, in theſe Kingdoms, many Eſtates, as well as many Farms, in a ſtate of good management; they being either under the immediate direction of Proprietors, who have turned their attention to rural concerns; or of Agents, who have a practical knowledge of Rural Affairs, and who have no intereſts ſubverſive of, or diſtinct from, the good order and proſperity of the Eſtates under their care. But there will be little riſk in ſaying, that a majority of the larger Eſtates, throughout the Iſland, are under very different principles of management.

I am equally deſirous to be explicit, with reſpect to SOCIETIES OF AGRICULTURE. I have ſaid in another place (ſee the RURAL ECONOMY of the MIDLAND COUNTIES, Vol. I. P. 121.), that mixed Societies are capable of producing good, by aſſimilating the ſentiments of Proprietors and Occupiers. And I believe that Provincial Societies have ever been beneficial, *in the outſet*, to the Diſtricts in which they have been formed, by agitating the Subject, and tending to awaken the SPIRIT OF IMPROVEMENT.

The fubjects, that would naturally offer themfelves to fuch Affociations, are the following.

25.

ASSOCIA-
TIONS OF
LANDED
GENTLE-
MEN.

The prefent management of landed property, in the Diftrict of Affociation.

The laying out of eftates, into farm lands, or fuch as are adapted to cultivation, and into woodlands, or fuch as are fitteft for the production of timber or coppice wood.

The fuitable fizes and characters of farms.

The fpecies of tenancy.

The forms of leafes.

The qualifications of tenants.

The proper feafons and terms of removals, receiving rents, &c. &c.

The encouragement of good managers, and the difcountenancing of bad ones.

The permanent improvement of farm lands, by draining, watering, &c. And their more temporary melioration, by manures, fodburning, tillage, &c.

The plan, and conftruction, of farm yards, and buildings.

VOL. II.   X   The

25.

ASSOCIA·
TIONS OF
LANDED
GENTLE-
MEN.

The management of hedges.

The management of timber, woodlands, and plantations.

And the more general improvement of the given Diſtrict of Aſſociation ;—by

Public Embankments.

Public Drains.

Public Navigations.

Public Incloſures.

The melioration of Tithes, and

The Poor's Rate : as well as the regulation of

County concerns ; and the ſupport of

The landed Intereſt ; which has lain neglected and trampled on, by Commerce and Manufactures, until the Country is no longer able to provide ſuſtinence for its inhabitants *

SEPTEMBER

* For a ſtriking evidence of the truth of this aſſertion, ſee the RURAL ECONOMY of the MIDLAND COUNTIES, Vol.II. P. 294.

26.

1792. SEPT. 24. The MONASTERY
BARN of this place is perhaps the firſt to
be found, at this day, in the Iſland : not in
reſpect to ſize, though it is large, but in
regard to the ſtate of preſervation,—both
of its walls, and its roof.

This Barn, having been built under the
Pack-horſe plan of Huſbandry, was moſt
inconvenient for carriages ; having only one
pair of doorways, in the middle of it ;
with a paſſage through, and a thraſhing
floor on either ſide of the roadway. The
width of the barn (namely, twentyſeven
feet in the clear), not permitting waggons
to turn within the area, the Corn has ever
been thrown, from the waggons, upon the
floors, and thence flung, from hand to
hand, to either end of the barn ! which is
a hundred and fifty feet in length.

The obvious method of improvement
was to break out doorways, towards the

X 2	ends;

26.

BARN OF
BUCKLAND.

ends; fo as to divide the whole length of
the barn, into fix bays or mowfteads, with
a floor between each two, in the *Englifh*
manner: an arduous tafk, which is now
executing; and which will render it one
of the firft barns in the Kingdom.

NATURE OF
CEMENT.

The labor of cutting thefe doorways is
nearly equal to that of cutting through
folid rock, of equal thicknefs; namely,
three feet. The cement is of an extraordinary quality: as hard almoft as granite;
efpecially on the North fide of the building. That of the South or rather South-
Weft wall is much more friable: a circumftance which has been obferved in other
old buildings of this place; and which is
entitled to Philofophic enquiry.

27.

THE USES
OF RILLS.

SEPTEMBER 24. A Spring in the upper
part of this Farm fupplies the houfe with
water. It alfo fupplies a drinking pool,

near

near the yards; and its natural courſe
carrying it through a ſmall Strawyard, a
trough is placed acroſs the rill, for the uſe
of the yard cattle.

27.

It has alſo, time immemorial, been led
over ſome graſs lands, which lie below the
yards,—on the float-and-drain principle.

But although this rill is ſeldom if ever
dried up—leading it along the ſides of the
Valley, through upland incloſures, which
are deſtitute of water for ſtock, and their
value of courſe thereby much depreciated,
—does not appear to have been thought of.

In the courſe of laſt Summer, being deſirous to know if this rill could be carried
through an intended ſuite of yards, on the
ſide of the Valley, I took the level, and
found not only that objeƈt to be attainable,
but alſo that it may be led with eaſe into
two waterleſs fields, which lie above theſe
yards; and, through them, into four or
five more (equally in want of water for
ſtock), ſituated beyond them.

In aſcertaining theſe facts, I made uſe of
a maſon's long level, inverted: a plummet

X 3   hole

hole being previously cut in the head of the standard; the crown of which being set upon the ground, the arms of the level were steadied by rods, in the horizontal position; and a carpenter's rule held across another rod, set up, at as great a distance as a clear sight would admit of, and at a height upon the staff, equal to the height of the level.

Finding this a most simple and perfect instrument, but difficult to adjust, by reason of its instability, I have since had a FRAME LEVEL made, on the same principle; namely, with a straight edge, or top rail, answering to the base board of the long level; with a broad piece falling down from the middle of it, answering to the standard; and with two end pieces or legs, to supersede the use of the rods; together with a bottom rail, eight or nine inches from the ground, and with diagonal braces, to keep the whole firm, and prevent the middle or plumb line from getting out of the square, with the straight edge of the top rail; which is seven or eight feet long, and

and the height about four feet *. And, as
an improvement of the rule and rod, I
contrived a CROSS STAFF; namely, a flip
of thin deal about five feet and a half long,
with a crofs piece, about two feet long and
three inches wide, fixed in the edge of it,
at the exact height of the level; the top
of the ftaff rifing twelve or eighteen inches
above the upper edge of the crofs piece,
that the hand of the perfon who holds it up
may not interfere with the view †.

With this inftrument, I have lately traced
the FLOWING LEVEL of the intended rill,
for watering the yards, and the grounds
beforementioned.

To afcertain the proper fall of a rill of
this intention, I previoufly took the running level of the antient floating Leat of
the meadows ‡; and finding its fall irre-

X 4   gular,

27.

CONSTRUC-
TION OF A
NEW LEVEL

CONDUCT-
ING MADE
RILLS.

---

* Half a rod long, and a quarter of a rod high, are eligible dimenfions, when great accuracy is required. But
a fhorter length, as one third of a rod, is more handy.

† This crofs piece fhould be of white wood, as deal,
or be painted white, that it may be the more diftinctly
feen, at a diftance.

‡ See Vol. I. P. 206.

27.

CONDUCT-
ING MADE
RILLS.

gular, I took it in two places, where the variations were greateſt. In the firſt, the fall was twentyſeven inches, in one hundred and ten feet; which is nearly one inch, or one foot, of fall, to fifty inches, or fifty feet, in length. In this part the current is in a degree rapid; the fall much too great for the general intention. The fall, in one hundred and ten feet of the other part, is barely ſix inches; which is only one meaſure of perpendicular height to two hundred and twenty of horizontal length. But in this part, the motion is too ſluggiſh : the ſurface of the water is nearly ſmooth ; barely dimpling; no ripple, or agitation appears. The fall is evidently too little for a water courſe, in which there is not a conſtant ſtream.

PROPER
FALL OF
RILLS.

I have therefore fixed upon ⅎNE MEASURE IN A HUNDRED, as the proper fall of a water courſe, into which water is occaſionally thrown; for the purpoſes of watering lands, filling drinking pools, ciſterns, &c. &c.

To adjuſt the level to this deſcent, I meaſured one hundred feet in length, and having

having nicely afcertained the DEAD LEVEL, I depreffed the range of the top bar, one foot below the upper edge of the crofs piece of the ftaff, and, while in that pofition, I marked the fituation of the plumb line, on the face of the level; the plummet hole being made wide for this purpofe: thus *fixing* the FLOWING LEVEL.

With this defcent, I have traced a line, from an intended refervoir, and from point to point, through the fields of one fide of the farm, and find that it reaches, even with this defcent, within every field: and that three fourths, or a larger proportion, of the furface are *capable* of being floated, from this intended pool.

To fee the actual motion of water falling one in a hundred, I have had fifty yards of the upper end of the line opened, and find the current fully fufficient; a lively rippling ftream; more active perhaps than is necef-fary. But the leakage being the lefs, the quicker the water moves, we may fafely conclude, that one foot of fall in a hundred feet of length is nearly perfect.

By

27.

PROPER
FALL OF
RILLS.

By the fame means, I have alfo found that, from a fimilar refervoir to be formed near the fource of the rill, water might be conveyed to every field, and almoft every acre of the oppofite fide of the farm.

USES OF
RESERVOIRS.

The ufes of thefe refervoirs will be thofe of having in readinefs, during the fummer months, when the rill is weak, a body of water to throw into drinking pools, cifterns, &c.: a weak current turned into a dry trench is abforbed by its perforations and fiffures, for fometime, at leaft, after it is turned in: whereas a body of water, rufhing quickly along it, not only in part efcapes abforption, but tends to fill up the leaks : and, in winter, thefe refervoirs will be ufeful in fcouring the trenches, and in hoarding up bodies of water, for the purpofe of irrigation.

In fetting out thefe rills, I have laid the head or upper end of each, from two to three feet below the intended furfaces of their refpective refervoirs, when full. Hence, by means of a portcullis floodgate, a body of water, two or three feet deep,

and

and the whole extent of the furfaces of the
bafons, may be poured into the rills, fafter
or flower, as occafion may require.

28.

SEPTEMBER 30. The Florifts of this
Diftrict have an effectual and ready way
of DESTROYING EARTH WORMS, in their
knots and borders; by the means of an infufion of wallnut-tree leaves. The procefs
is this:---fill a veffel nearly full, with leaves,
gathered in the firft or fecond week of
September;---cover them with water, and
let them ftand two or three days, until the
water has acquired a blackifh green color.
With this infufion, the beds and alleys are
watered, by means of the common watering
pot. The worms prefently, rife to the
furface, and die in apparent agony.

It ftrikes me that this interefting fact
may be turned to a profitable purpofe, in
the forming of DRINKING POOLS. It is
probable,

28.

DRINKING
POOLS.

probable, that leaves of the walnut, fpread under the clay, would have the fame effect as the lime, which is now in ufe *

Reflecting on this fubject, it appears to me further probable, that the ufe of clay, in making pools, may be difpenfed with. Thus :---form the bafon ; puddle with the beft of the excavated mold; ftrew on leaves; and pave with liquid mortar ; made up with their infufion,---if required.

The bafon form of the pit is an objection to puddling ; and could not, perhaps, be effected otherways, than progreffively with the pavement , by puddling above each ring, and bedding the ftones in the medi-cated matter; pouring in liquid cement, where it might appear to be wanted. Or, perhaps, the medicated batter would in itfelf be fufficient.

This is a fubject of great importance, in upland fituations. Forming drinking pools with clay and lime (great as was the dif-covery) is difficult and expenfive ; and any means of fimplifying the procefs would be valuable. SEP

* See YORK. ECON. Vol. I. P. 146.

29.

LAYING OUT
FARMERIES.

SEPTEMBER 30. FARM BUILDINGS. Where a blank is given, — where the ground may be chofen,—where there are no buildings already erected,—or, where there are given buildings, if they ftand in the defired fituation.—few difficulties can arife, in laying out a Farmery.

But where the fite is given, — where there are principal buildings already fixed on the fpot,—and thefe on aukward ground, and in aukward fituations with refpect to each other, as they are on this farm, it requires great ftudy and invention to render the yards and additional buildings convenient, or commodious.

FARMERY
OF
BUCKLAND.

In this cafe, the capital barn, already mentioned, is fituated between the dwelling houfe, and a range of fpacious office buildings,— on the fide of a fteep hill ; the

out

29.

FARMERY
OF
BUCKLAND.

out buildings above,---the houfe below---
the barn ;---with other offices, at a confiderable diftance.

The defirable object, here, was to collect
the whole into a compact form, in the immediate vicinity of the barn. And this
has been effected, by forming a femi-
octagon yard, in the front of the principal
range of buildings ; and inclofing it with a
line of cattle fheds ; the area of the yard
being formed into a receptacle for the dung
of the fheds and ftables.

This form of a farm yard, though I have
been led to it by circumftances, cannot perhaps be improved ; even where a blank
fite is given ; except by that of a compleat
octagon.

CATTLE
YARDS.

An OCTAGONAL YARD is warm, and
is much more commodious than a fquare
one ; by reafon of the fharp inconvenient
angles being cut off; and octagonal fheds
are equally commodious ; each fide having
its range of ftalls, with fodder houfes in the
angles, between them : a gangway, in this
cafe, running from end to end, before the
heads of the cattle, and through the ftore
houfes ;

houfes; which have doors opening to the road, on the back or outer fide of the fheds, to receive the food ;---whether it be hay, ftraw, roots, or other material.

30.

OCTOBER 5. The doors of the ftore houfes of thefe fheds are hung to open outward ; to prevent a wafte of room, and to render them more fecure againft intruders. To increafe the fecurity, they are hung with a fall to the catch ; and to prevent their being injured by the weather, when open, they have alfo a fall, backward, under the eaves of the building. To effect this, the balance point is placed in the midway, between the two extreme pofitions of the door ; which, being fet at right angle to the line of the building, has a fall to either hand *

The

* See MID. ECON. Vol. II. P. 79. for practical rules on this fubject.

30.

HANGING
DOORS.

The hooks and catches are laid into blocks of moorſtone, and worked up into the jambs of the doorways; the material of building being a coarſe ſchiſtus, or ſlate ſtone.

The hooks of the new doorways of the barn I am likewiſe laying into moorſtone; receſſes being hewn out of the jambs to receive the blocks; which are large, and fixed firmly in their places;---firſt, by means of wedge-ſhaped ſtones, driven in above them; and, afterwards, by wedging them in more firmly, with thin pieces of iron; forcing out the cement, at every crevice.

AN EFFECT
OF RUST?

It is obſervable, that the hooks of the original doors of the barn, which are in like manner laid in ſtone, have moſt of them burſt their bounds, and broken off more or leſs of the outer parts of the ſtones they are reſpectively laid in. A ſenſible and ex‧perienced ſtone maſon is of opinion, that theſe fractures are occaſioned by the ruſting of the iron; having, he ſays, carefully traced the effect, in ſeveral inſtances.

But

But may not this effect be caused by the susceptibility of metals, with respect to heat and cold? Or may not the mischiefs, in the instance under notice, have been done by the jarring of the heavy doors, blown violently to, by the wind? I have, however, observed similar fractures, in cases where the last suggested cause could not so easily operate.

Facts, which require a succession of ages to produce them, are too interesting to be passed without attention. The effect here noticed is observable in many ancient buildings, and the operation of the rust of iron is not, perhaps, accurately understood.

30.

AN EFFECT OF RUST.

31.

October 13. Doors hung on hooks laid into the wall, as above described, require to be hung in *rabbets*. For, if they are hung in *between* the jambs, rain and snow will beat in: if they *lap over*, on the

HANGING DOORS.

31.

HANGING
DOORS.

outſide, they are expoſed to the weather, are in harm's way, and are unſightly. A rabbet, of due dimenſions, obviates theſe inconveniences. And I have found that, for ledge doors, made of inch boards, and hung to fall back under the eaves, in the manner above mentioned, three inches deep, each way, are the proper dimenſions.

32.

LIMING
LAND.

OCTOBER 28. Laſt year, I had the lime, for wheat, ſet about the field, in waggon-load heaps; with the intention of mixing with it the velled Beat, or the aſhes that might ariſe from it, as the ſeaſon ſhould render moſt convenient. But I left the Country, before I had an opportunity of ſeeing the operation, properly performed.

This year, ſimilar heaps being ſet about, I have had them covered, thickly, with unburnt Beat, collected with the team rake, or " drudge," of the Country; and the
whole

whole duly " melled" or mixt, in the
Devonſhire manner *; with a ſmall deviation in this caſe.

The operation being purpoſely begun
before the middles of the heaps were fallen,
they were firſt pulled abroad, with a hack ;
thus giving a rough mixture to the un-
ſlacked knobs of lime and the wet Beat,
under which they were deeply buried.
This brought on a quick diſſolution of the
lime ; whoſe heat, of courſe, operated in the
deſtruction of weed ſeeds and animalculæ ;
and, while the heat was at its height, the
whole were intimately mixed together ;
thus ſaving, by one eaſy proceſs, the endleſs
labor of two tedious operations.

33.

OCTOBER 28. (See MIN. 27.) In conducting this rill through an open grove of
tall trees, I have found ſome difficulties :
not only the *ground* but the *trees* were

Y 2   given.

* See the Article LIME, Vol. I. Page 158.

given. By purfuing the following methods, thefe difficulties have been overcome.

Having, by means of the frame level and crofs, afcertained the general defcent, or flowing level, through the whole extent of the grove ; and having, in this operation, gained a general idea of the requifite direction of the rill, by means of ftakes placed at the feveral ftations of the crofs ftaff, wherever clear views could be caught through the openings between the trees,— the intermediate fpaces, between the ftakes, were traced by the eye, fo as to endeavour to follow the natural level of the ground, without forming abrupt bends in the channel ;—parrying between the two.

The fuppofed line being thus fet out, the furface of the ground was cleared two or three feet wide on either fide of it, from leaves and other incumbrances, and the top foil removed for manure ; thus making a hollow pathway through the grove, fome four or five feet wide.

The next operation was to level this pathway ; which was likewife done by the eye, from ftake to ftake ; paring off the

pro-

protuberances, and cafting or wheeling them into the hollows.

To come at the true line, and to render the flowing level perfectly uniform, a narrow pathlet, the width of the fpade, was formed on the upper fide of the broad pathway. This pathlet was formed, with the frame level in hand; finking trenches in the ftill protuberating parts, and raifing banklets in the hollows: thus *fixing* the exact flowing level, at each level's length; and, at the fame time, forming the face, or lower fide of it, in fuch manner as to eafe the bends, and give a fmooth flowing line to the rill.

In order to bring the bufinefs of forming the bed of the rill to a certainty, and thereby to render any further fuperintendance unneceffary, yet to prevent error in the execution, I formed a gauge for the laborers to work by.

This gauge confifts of a board, forming the fegment of a circle; the chord or greateft length being three feet, the greateft depth twelve inches. This gives the dimenfions of the bed of the rill. To keep

Y 3   the

the bottom of it, exactly true to the flowing level, fo that the current or ftream may be perfectly uniform, — this gauge is fixed under a mafon's fhort level ; the end of one of the arms projecting, three or four inches, beyond one end of the gauge.

The trench being funk, to nearly its proper depth, by the eye, kept on the adjufted margin, the projecting end of the level is placed on the fame marginal guide, and the plummet line being brought to the perpendicular (and the bafe of the level of courfe rendered horizontal), the bottom of the trench is finifhed, *with certainty*.

This evening, I have had the water turned into the upper part of the trench thus formed, by two common laborers, who never before, perhaps, took a level in their hands. The current is not only defirable, as to defcent; but is perfectly uniform,—*without alteration*.

Hence the practicability and certainty of this method of forming the channels of rills,—as well as the eligibility of one meafure in a hundred, for the defcent or fall,--- are fully afcertained.

The

The dimensions above stated,—namely, three feet wide and one foot deep,—(a size fully sufficient for any purposes, at present intended by this rill) I have adopted as the fittest for the part which passes under trees, and which will be liable to be choaked by leaves and falling twigs. But a part which crosses an open grass ground, and where cattle will frequently pass and repass, I have had formed by a shallower gauge: namely, a segment four feet wide and eight inches deep; the bank on the lower side of it being made broad, and flatly convex; to prevent the cattle from treading in the sides: and, to give it more immediate firmness, it is turfed with the sods, taken from the part which is now the bed of the rill.

DECEMBER 8. The laying out and forming of ROADS have engrossed a principal part of my attention, during the last two or three weeks; and, so far as relates

Y 4   to

33.
CONDUCT-
ING RILLS.

LAYING OUT
ROADS.

to convex roads, on a defcent, I have brought this ufeful art to method and a degree of certainty.

In the forming of roads, as in the conducting of rills, the frame level and crofs are accurate and ready guides.

The given points of the intended road having been marked, the moft defirable line, whether as to utility or ornament, is to be fet out, with tall ftakes placed at equal diftances, as ten paces from each other. Thefe preparatory fteps having been taken fome days previous to the commencement of the work,—in order to give time for deliberate adjuftments,—the level and the crofs are placed at the oppofite extremities of the line, or as near them as a clear fight can be caught from the one to the other; and the level being deliberately adjufted to the crofs, the fituation of the plumb line is marked, on the face of the level; and thus the rake or degree of DESCENT is determined and *fixed*; and, of courfe, a uniformity of defcent, if required, may thereby be accurately preferved, in every part of the line. If this wind much,

the

the degree of inclination or defcent will be diminifhed, as the length of line is encreafed; and, if an exact uniformity be required, an allowance fhould be made for fuch deviation. But, if the declivity be long, relaxations in the line of afcent, at fuitable diftances, have their ufe for heavy carriages, and are not difpleafing to the eye.

The degree of defcent being determined, the next ftep is to try if the line marked out correfpond with it. This is done by keeping the level in its place, and fetting up the crofs at the foot of each ftake, or at the feet of as many as occafion requires.

If the marked line deviate, much, from the line of general level; fo as to render the road inconvenient, or encreafe, unneceffarily, the expence of making it, a frefh line is fet out; endeavouring to parry, between the true line of direction, and the true line of defcent.

The line of direction being finally determined on, and adjufted, a ftrong ftump, or flender pile, two feet or more in length, is entered, with an iron crow, at the foot of each ftake; and driven down to the
general

general rake of the intended furface of the
road, when finifhed.

This is readily done, by placing the feet
of the level, on this intended line of furface,
and putting the foot of the crofs upon the
head of each ftump; continuing to keep
the level to the rake line, and to drive the
ftump, until the arms of the crofs are feen
to range exactly, with the ftraight edge of
the level; or, which is frequently more
expeditious, efpecially where the fubfoil is
ftoney, by placing the foot of the crofs
againft the fide of the pile, and raifing or
lowering it, until the raking level be caught;
then marking, and fawing off, the head of
the ftump: proceeding in this manner,
until each ftake is fupplanted by a pile.

Where the ground is very rough and
uneven, it is convenient to break down the
protuberances, by the eye, previoufly to
the adjuftment of the piles.

The piles being adjufted, a regular
trench or pathway is formed, the whole
length of the line of road fet out, at a depth
below the heads of the ftumps, equal to
the intended thicknefs of the covering
materials:

materials : namely, in private roads and ordinary cafes, one foot : leaving the piles ftanding in the middle of the trench or pathway ; fhowing one foot of their length above the intended bed of the road, with another foot, or a fufficient length in the ground, to keep them firmly in their places, until the road be finifhed ; the heads of the piles being the requifite guide to the covering.

This trench or pathway being the true middle line of the bed of the road, an unerring guide is given to the workman, and the bufinefs of the artift is at an end. The reft is mere labor, which may be performed, by ordinary workmen, under general directions.

The BED OF THE ROAD I make flat, or nearly fo ; the outer edges, only, dipping fomewhat beneath the general level ; the convexiture of the road, itfelf, being given with the rough foundation materials.

35.

1793. JANUARY 29. There are, now, on this demefne, fortyfive acres of over-grown COPPICE WOOD; namely, wood of about thirty years growth.

The lands of this Diftrict being in general unfriendly to the Oak, after it attains a certain growth, much of the fpray and upper branches of this wood are beginning to decay. Inftead of encreafing in value, it is probably getting worfe, every year;—efpecially with refpect to its bark, which is at prefent a valuable part of it. Twenty years, I find, is the ufual growth of coppice wood, here, and every circumftance weighed, it is perhaps, on the whole, the moft eligible.

The ufual price of coppice wood, at twenty years growth, has been of late years ten to twelve pounds, the " cuftomary acre"

acre" of the country * ; for wood growing
on land of a quality, equal to that of arable
lands, which are worth ten or twelve ſhillings the *ſtatute* acre. Of courſe, woodlands afford, to their proprietors, little more
than half the annual rent of farm lands, of
equal quality.

For ſuppoſe coppice wood of twenty years
growth ſells for ten pounds the provincial
acre,—this is but barely equivalent to ſeven
ſhillings an acre, received annually for farm
lands ; as, in the courſe of twenty years,
the intereſt of the ſeveral annual ſums received, and the accumulating intereſt there-
upon ariſing, amounts to nearly half the
principal : and, if a farther reduction be
made for the difference between the provincial and the ſtatute acre, we ſhall bring
down this nominal rent of ten ſhillings, an
acre, a year, to little more than five.

Twenty pounds, an acre, have been
offered for twenty acres of the beſt of this
coppice wood; under the conditions of
being

---

* The "CUSTOMARY ACRE" of this Diſtrict is calculated on eighteen feet to the perch: five provincial acres
being about equal to ſix ſtatute acres.

35.

RENTAL
VALUE.

being allowed two years for the felling of it ; — and to pay at Chriſtmas for the quantity taken down in the preceding year ; agreeably to the uſual cuſtom of the Diſtrict.

This farther delay of the receipt of the principal, and the attendant loſs of intereſt, is a farther reduction of the annual rent of the land ; yet is ſeldom, perhaps, taken into the account, in calculating the net produce of woodlands.

On calculation, I find that twenty pounds an acre, for wood of thirty years growth, does not neat more than ſeven ſhillings and nine pence an acre, received annually, and put out, at ſimple intereſt, at five percent. At four percent, and reckoning nothing for intereſt on the accumulating intereſt (which in a courſe of years would amount to a conſiderable ſum), this price does not neat more than eight ſhillings and five pence an acre, a year, received annually as rent; even ſuppoſing the whole money to be paid down at the time of ſale.

RECLAIMING
COPPICE
GROUND.

About thirty acres of this tract of wood-land lies on a culturable ſlope ; and would
be

be worth, in a ſtate of full cultivation, fifteen to twenty ſhillings an acre : whereas,
in a ſtate of woodland, it has probably
never paid more than one third of the
money ; and is not, in reality, worth more
than half of it.

The propriety of reclaiming it, from its
preſent unprofitable ſtate, admits not of
diſpute ; and the means of bringing it into
cultivation is the only point which remains
to be determined.

To dig up the roots entirely, ſo as to
admit the plow, in the firſt inſtance, would
not only be expenſive ; but, by bringing
up the ſubſtrata, the cultivated ſoil would
be debaſed, and rendered unproductive for
a courſe of years.

But, by clearing away the whole, level
with the ground, or a little within the ſurface of it ; and dreſſing this freed ſurface
with lime, in order to diſſolve, the more
readily, the leaves and decayed wood with
which it is thickly covered ; and by giving
a degree of evenneſs to the ſurface with
the harrow and the roller ; ſowing ſuitable
graſs ſeeds between the operations ; a ſheep
walk

walk would be immediately obtained ; and, in a few years, when the roots were decayed, and a turf formed over them, the land might be broken up with eafe and profit *.

36.

COPPICE
WOOD.

FEBRUARY 13. (See the laft MINUTE.) A few days ago, I fold the whole of this coppice wood, at the high price of twenty two pounds ten fhillings an acre ; and under the following favorable conditions †.

CONDITIONS
OF SALE.

The whole to be taken down in two years ; namely, in the years 1793 and 1794.

* For former Remarks on this Method of Reclaiming Woodlands, fee YORK. ECON. Vol. I. page 316.

† Thefe Conditions are inferted, here, for the general purpofe of giving the Reader an opportunity of comparing them with thofe of other Diftricts ; and to affift, eventually, in drawing Forms of CONDITIONS OF SALES ; which, as FORMS OF LEASES, are at prefent, in a degree vague and unfixed.

1794.—One hundred pounds of the purchafe money to be paid down each year, previoufly to the commencement of the cutting; one moiety of the remainder of the amount of what fhall be taken down in each year, at Midfummer; the other moiety at the enfuing Chriftmas The purchafer to be allowed a fquare perch for each tree ftanding among the coppice wood, and a quarter of a perch, for each ftandle of the laft cutting. To finifh the cuttings, by Midfummer, and to clear the ground, by the Chriftmas following, in each year, &c. &c.

Previoufly to this advantageous bargain, I had an offer of twenty pounds an acre, for the whole, to be taken down in five years.

The difference between thefe two prices appears, on a fuperficial view of them, to be little more than a hundred pounds. But if the intereft of money, and the growth of the fucceeding wood be taken into the calculation, the fuperior advantages of the latter will be found to amount to more than two hundred pounds: as appears in the following ftatement.

36.

CONDITIONS
OF SALE.

SALE OF
COPPICE
WOOD.

Vol. II.   Z   Firft,

36.

SALE OF
COPPICE
WOOD.

First, forty five acres, at 20l. an acre, and taking down nine acres a year.

	Princ.	Int.		£.	s.	d.
	£.	£.				
1ſt Year,	180	00	Growth of Wood at 8s.	3	12	0
2d	180	9	——————	7	4	0
3d	180	18	——————	10	16	0
4th	180	27	——————	14	8	0
5th	180	36	——————	18	0	0
	900 Prin.	90		54	0	0
	90 Intereſt					
	54 Growth of Wood.					

£.1044 the total Advantage, at the end of five years.

Secondly, forty five acres at 22l. 10s. and twenty two and a half acres, a year.

	Princ.			Int.				£.	s.	d.
	£.	s.	d.	£.	s.	d.				
1ſt Year,	506	5	0	00	0	0	Growth of Wood,	9	0	0
2d	506	5	0	25	6	3	—————	18	0	0
3d	00	0	0	50	12	6	—————	18	0	0
4th	00	0	0	50	12	6	—————	18	0	0
5th	00	0	0	50	12	6	—————	18	0	0
	1012	10	0	177	3	9		81	0	0
	177	3	9 Intereſt							
	81	0	0 Growth of Wood.							

1270 13 9 total Advantage at the end of five years.
1044 0 0 as above

£.226 13 9 ſuperior Advantage *.

F͟ᴇʙʀᴜᴀʀʏ

* Theſe Statements are publiſhed, for the inſtruction of thoſe, to whom calcul. tions of this kind may not be familiar. The uſe of them is obvious.

37.

FEBRUARY 14. The fide walls of an SECURING BUILDINGS. ancient monaſtic building having fled from the upright, — by the buttreſſes in front having given way at the foundation, and by the back wall being impelled forward, by a load of earth and a road, behind it,— (the ground, on the outſide, being ſeveral feet higher than on the inſide) I have ſecured, in the manner hereafter deſcribed.

What rendered this caſe the more difficult was the circumſtance of both walls requiring ſupport; yet both of them inclining the ſame way; ſo that there was no *tie* to be got, nor any *purchaſe* to be had.

If the front wall had been ſtayed, by freſh buttreſſes; ſtill the back wall (againſt which the preſſure immediately acted) would have remained, in a degree unſupported. There are, in this, as in other Gothic buildings, no binding beams to the roof; nor any other tie between the two

Z 2   walls,

37.

walls, than the floor beams of a chamber. Befide, buttrefses, in front, would have been inconvenient, and unfightly; and, like other fupports on the *outfides* of buildings, would have been liable to the drip of the eaves, and to the effects of the weather.

The expedient, which I hit upon, was that of raifing ftrong buttresses, on the inside of the building, againft the back wall; which is thus firmly ftayed, and effectually prevented from farther inclination; and, at the fame time, firm purchafes are obtained, for the purpofe of tying in the front wall; which has been done in fuch a manner as will probably be the means of prolonging the duration of the building,—a few more ages of time.

The ties, in this cafe, are large oak floor-beams; which are fecurely fixed, in front, to the old buttreffes; and, to the back wall, by means of large blocks of granite or moorftone; in fhape, the lower fruftums of fquare pyramids. Thefe blocks are laid in, flufh with the outfide of the wall, and with their bafes outward; beds or receffes having been accurately cut out of the

rocklike

rocklike fubftance of the wall, to receive them.

Through thefe blocks, pafs ftrong iron bars, or pins; which are firmly ftrapped to the ends of the beams (bearing on the tops of the buttreffes); and which are fecured, and the ties drawn tight, by means of ftrong wedges or keys, drawing againft broad firm difks of iron, bearing againft the perforated blocks; which thus operate as dovetails to the ties.

In building thefe buttreffes, the foun-dations, as well as each courfe of ftones, were made to dip towards the wall, in the fame proportion as the buttreffes incline, or batter: the courfes being kept at right angle to the line of batter, or face of the buttrefs:—a principle which ought not to be deviated from. For, by adhering to it, the refiftance is rendered the greateft; and, by placing the buttrefs in a falling pofture, towards the wall, it fettles the more firmly againft it; while, by toothing the one into the other, as has been done in this cafe, the whole fettles, intimately and firmly, into one incorporate mafs.

Z 3　　　　F EBRUARY

38.

FEBRUARY 16. On a farm on which SHEEP are a principal object, TEMPORARY LEYS productive of sheep feed become, likewise, an object of the first magnitude. The practice of mowing, the first year, leys intended for five or six years duration, is a crime for which nothing, but necessity, is admissible as an excuse. By this improvident step, the sward or turf is rendered thin of plants, for several succeeding years. Not only the more delicate species of herbage, which seldom fail to rise after a short course of aration, are liable to be checked or smothered, by the luxuriant growth, and impervious shade, of cultivated herbage; but the cultivated herbs, themselves, are in some certain degree weakened, and their number decreased; especially if the soil be much exhausted, or be out of tilth.

On

On this farm, a ftriking inftance of the mifchief arifing from the practice of mowing fuch leys, the firft year, is at this time moft evident. The young ley grounds, which were mown laft fummer, may be faid to be now unoccupied ; except by daifies, groundfel, and a few other weeds. One of them, though the land is of a fuperior quality, is not worth, for the coming year, five fhillings an acre. Whereas, had it been paftured down, clofe, laft fpring and fummer, it would, in all probability, have been worth five times that rent---for this and feveral fucceeding years,---as a fheep pafture.

To every farm, on which cultivated leys, of five or fix years duration, make a part of the plan of management, the moft defirable appendage is a fufficiency of MEADOW LANDS, or PERENNIAL MOWING GROUNDS, to furnifh the farm with a fupply of hay, without being under the neceffity of mowing temporary leys, the firft year; and happily circumftanced is the farm, whofe fituation, with refpect to the quality and quantity of water it commands, enables it

to

38.

TEMPORA-
RY GRASS-
LANDS.

PLAN OF
FARMING.

38.

to produce, by IRRIGATION, a fufficiency of hay, to carry its requifite liveftock, through the winter months.

The demefne lands of this eftate are for-tunately in this fituation. Some twenty or thirty acres of them have been more or lefs watered, time immemorial; and with water of a fuperior quality.

The effects of the flate-rock waters of this Diftrict are fuperior to thofe of any others I have had an opportunity of obfer-ving; the chalk waters of Wiltfhire and Hampfhire excepted. There are flopes of hills on this and the furrounding farms, which are now as green and *grofs*, to the eye at a diftance, as the rankeft wheat in May *.

Seeing thefe advantages, I have been affiduous to afcertain the facts refpecting the poffibility of watering the different parts of this eftate; and I found, fome time ago (fee MIN. 27.), that almoft every acre of it is *capable* of being flooded, artificially, by running water. The QUANTITY OF

WATER,

---

* It is everywhere obfervable, and is moft interefting, that the fteeper the flope, the more obvious is the effect.

WATER, however, that can be conveyed to it, though fufficient to furnifh pafturing ftock, with a valuable fupply of beverage, is too fmall for the purpofes of irrigation.

But the mifchiefs arifing from the prac‑ tice of mowing ley grounds, the firft year, having lately preffed more clofely on my mind, I have been ftudying, with redoubled‑ attention, the capacity of the different grounds of this farm, with refpect to water. And I have difcovered, that a fufficiency of them, to anfwer, fully, the purpofes re‑ quired, are capable of receiving an abundant fupply of water; and that fuch a fupply may be brought to them, at a fmall ex‑ pence.

But the waters which are already within the farm, claiming the firft attention, I have, hitherto, been endeavouring to turn them to the beft advantage; by conducting them properly over the lands which moft command them.

This has been effected by taking the water out of its natural channel, at different heights, and conveying it to the feveral ftages of the flopes, over which thefe lands

are

38.

are fpread, by means of main floats, leats, or
artificial rills, for the purpofe of feeding the
floating trenches, which diftribute and
fpread the water over the faces of the
flopes.

In fetting out and forming thefe conducting channels, I have found the frame
level and crofs fafe and ready affiftants ;
and the defcent of one meafure in a hundred
moft eligible ;—as giving a lively motion
to the water, and a firm bottom to the channel, without wearing away its fides.

In conducting channels of this intention,
acrofs grounds much varied in furface, and
where a degree of ornament is required to
be joined with ufe, as was the cafe in this
inftance, fome attention is requifite.   If the
ground be implicitly followed with the
level, not only a circuitous length of channel and a wafte of land, but fhort angular
unfightly bends, are produced.   If, on the
contrary, ftraight lines are attempted acrofs
a varied furface, the labor of raifing the
hollows, and finking the knolls, is great,
and the beauty of the line is wholly loft.
Hence, where the ground does not naturally

rally afford the given line, the MIDDLE
COURSE is requifite to be chofen.

In this inftance of practice, I have found
it beft to fet out the line, firft by the level,
crooked or ftraight, as the ground directs;
then, to give it the required direction, by
the eye; and, afterward, to correct the eye
with the plummet; left the line fhould lie
much too high or too low, in any particular
part:—for a fteepfided trench is liable to
be trodden in by cattle, and a fharp ridgey
bank is equally liable to be torn down by
their tread: while, over a fhallow trench,
and a broad fwelling bank, they ftep
without injury.

But, in watering the hangs of hills where
a blank fite is given, and where no fences
already exift, there are few cafes, perhaps,
in which the main floats fhould be liable to
the paffage of ftock. The uppermoft is, of
courfe, laid as high as the flowing level
from the fource will allow, and neceffarily
divides the watered from the unwatered
lands; and is, of courfe, a *given* line of
fence. If the valley be narrow, or the
foot of the flope, which commands the
water,

water, be fhort, one main floating trench is fufficient. For by running parallel trench-lets along the face of the flope, at once to collect the difperfed waters, from above, and to diftribute them more evenly below; and by letting down a fupply of water to the lower trenchlets, when the upper fide of the flope is fufficiently watered; one main float is fufficient to fupply a field's width of land. And, if a continuation of the flope require it, another main float, and another fence, may, and in general ought to run parallel to the firft.

There are two reafons why fences of this fort fhould be placed on the *upper fide* of the floating rill. The water is more eafily let off, into the working trenches, than it would through a fence; and efpecially through a hedge; whofe roots, and the holes of the vermin they harbor, would be the caufe of a continual wafte of water.

Viewing fences, thus winding along the wavy furface of a flope, in the light of ornament, a light in which they ought to appear within this demefne, an additional motive, for running them along the fide of

a wavy

a wavy rill, arifes. If the broad fwelling
bank, which ought to accompany fuch a rill
on the lower fide, were formed into a
walk,—determined in width, and always
kept dry, by a working trench, on its lower
margin,—the bank would be rendered firm,
by the preffure of the foot, and, in this
inftance, a delightful ftroll will be obtained,
at an eafy coft.

38.
LAYING OUT
WATERED
LANDS.

39.

FEBRUARY 20. I have at length the
pleafure of feeing a TWO-OX PLOW compleatly in its work. Two oxen, in yoke,
with a fingle chain paffing from it, to the
draft iron of the plow, and driven, with
whip reins, by the plowman, have been
employed, during the laft fortnight, in
giving the firft fleet plowing of turnep
grounds : a work which they perform with
eafe and difpatch.

This is the fimpleft and cheapeft plow-
team

PLOWING
WITH
TWO OXEN.

team I have yet fet to work. The yoke
and fingle chain, if made light and well
fitted to the oxen, are, for a two-ox plow,
in light work, much preferable to collars,
traces, and fplinter bars; which are com-
plex, expenfive, and for ever entangling
with the reins; and the fplinter bars are a
heavy incumbrance, at the head of a light
fwing plow.

SEPTEMBER, 1794. This fummer, I
have had two of thefe admirable plow-
teams, in full work. employing them, chiefly,
in ftirring fallows; which they do with
great effect: plowing eight or nine inches
deep, with plows which clear their work.
To make the labor the lefs, and the operation the more effective, the flices are cut
narrow; not more than fix or feven inches
wide; by which means this cheap and eafy
plowing becomes nearly equal to fpade
work;—more effective than any number
of the partial plowings, ufually given to
broken ground, in this Diftrict.

MARCH

40.

MARCH 12. In the Autumn of 1791, FARMERY OF BUCK-LAND. I defigned and fet out, and have now brought into a train of finilhing, a fuite of FARM YARDS and BUILDINGS, on a large fcale. See MINUTE 29.

I have not leifure to regifter, in detail, the minutiæ of this improvement; but a few particulars ftrike.

A DUNG YARD of a femi-octagon form, inclofed, on one fide, with cattle fheds, and, on the other, by a line of ftables and farm offices; with oppofite gates and a carriage road, by the fide of the latter; is, in every point of view, in which I have yet feen it, very eligible.

CATTLE YARDS.

BATTERING FOUNDATION WALLS. The furface of this yard, by reafon of the form of the ground (fee page 317.), necef-farily rifes, in one part of it, nine or ten feet, above the road, which paffes on the outfide of the fheds confequently, the weight of

earth,

BUILDING.

40.
BUILDING.

earth, encreafed by the weight of the fheds, and that of the cattle they may contain, rendered it neceffary to counteract the inward preffure; and this has been effectually done, by carrying up the foundation of the back wall of the fheds, fo as to lean againft the load, and thereby act as a general buttrefs againft the preffure. This foundation wall leffens from four feet at the bafe, to two feet at the floor of the fheds, and level of the yard; not with a ftraight line of inclination; but with a gentle curvature, refembling that of the fpreading bafe of a well grown tree.

CATTLE
SHEDS.

The proper WIDTH of SHEDS, for full-grown cattle, with a three-feet paffage before their heads, is one ftatute rod (fixteen feet and a half) from out to out of the building; the back wall (in this cafe of ftone) being two feet thick.

The PILLARS of thefe fheds are of oak, and eight inches fquare, fet *upon* blocks of moorftone; out of which rife fhort iron pins, to keep the feet of the pofts in their places; the tops of the ftones declining gently from the pins; to prevent any water

from

from lodging upon them; and thereby to
elude, as much as poffible, the decay of the
timber.

The proper WIDTH OF A STALL, for
two middle-fized working oxen, is feven
feet. Cows, though of fmaller fize than
oxen, require as much or more room, for
the conveniency of milking them, and fuckling their calves. A danger of making
ftalls too wide is that of the cattle turning
round in them; and by that means placing
themfelves, in an aukward and dangerous
fituation, with refpect to their fellows.
This danger, however, is to be guarded
againft by a poft rifing in the middle of the
ftall, immediately before the fhoulders of
the cattle; in a line with the front pofts of
the PARTIAL PARTITIONS *: and a poft
in this place may be found ufeful to faften
calves to, during the time of fuckling.

The proper LENGTH OF STALLS, for
Devonfhire oxen, of the larger fize, is nine
feet; namely, three feet the width of the
trough, and fix feet the platform, or refting
VOL. II.   A a   place;

* See MID. ECON. Vol. I. P. 33.

place; with a depreffion, or defcent, of one
to two inches, from the outer rail of the
trough, to a break or drop in the pavement,
fix inches deep;—formed by ftrong flat
flate ftones, fet on edge; nearly perpendicularly, but fomewhat inclining to the
ftalls.

From the bottom of this break, to the
line formed by the bafe ftones of the pillars,
the PAVEMENT takes a gently convex or
fwelling form, and thence defcends, by a
continuation of the fame curve, to the
brink of the dung pit; into which, of
courfe, the water, falling from the eaves
of the fheds, readily finds its way.

On the higher fide of the yard, the DUNG
PIT fhelves, with a gentle defcent, from the
bafes of the pillars; but, on the lower fide,
it was found convenient to fink it, more
abruptly, from a broad path, or gangway
(fix feet wide from the pillars), to the
depth of three or four feet. The bank or
fteep fide of this dung pit is formed of the
fame flate ftones, as are the walls of the
fheds; not, however, perpendicularly, as
bank walls of this intention are frequently

carried

carried up; but very much battering, or falling back towards the sheds; the angle of inclination, from the perpendicular, being not less than thirty degrees. The foundation of this wall was dug, and the courses of stones laid, not horizontally, but at right angle, or square, with the line of reclination; the earth being firmly rammed in behind, as the wall was carried up. The uppermost or coping stones are large and strong; serving as bonds to the wall, and as a buttress to the convex pavement, above mentioned; which presses against these coping stones, on one side, and against those which form the outer edge of the platforms of the stalls, on the other, as an arch bears on its butments.

On a stage below this principal dung-yard, and on the upper side of the barn, a STRAWYARD, for loose cattle, and store swine, is shaped out of the slope of the hill on which this farmery is situated. And behind the range of offices, which form one side of the dung yard, is another straw yard. And between these two straw yards is a MILKING YARD.

These

40.

WATERING
YARDS.

Thefe three yards are WATERED, by means of the made rill, which has been fpoken of, in MINUTE 27; and which paffes through thefe yards, in channels, partially or wholly open, for the ufe of ftock; and thence through a covered drain, to its natural channel. In paffing through the principal ftrawyard, it runs along the top of a dwarf wall, or offset (at the foot of a fence wall), twelve or fifteen inches high, from the level of the yard; and about fourteen inches wide; with a channel, fix inches deep on the back part, fhelving upward to an angle in front; and divided by upright ftones, placed edgeway acrofs the rill; which has, here, a confiderable defcent: confequently, each obftruction forms an eddy, fmall pool, or drinking place; eight or ten head of cattle being able to drink, at the fame time, and with the moft perfect conveniency.

Finding, by experience, that too copious a fupply of water is, on many accounts, troublefome, in a rill of this intention, I afcertained the exact fize of the ftream required, by means of gauges of different dimenfions,

menſions, ſet acroſs the channel. And
having found, that a bore of two inches
diameter gave the deſired ſupply, I have
fixed a ſtone, perforated with a bore of this
diameter, in a penſtock, of oak, and placed
this acroſs the channel, above the yards,
with a waſte water channel, immediately
above it; ſo that an inordinate ſupply of
water, ſent down, by rains or otherwiſe, is
effectually prevented.

In this yard, the ſtall cattle are to be
watered, and to be allowed to amuſe themſelves, in the middle of the day; while the
ſtore ſwine are collecting in the dung yard,
whatever the ſtalls or the ſtables may afford
them; being carefully kept out of that
yard, while the cattle are in their ſtalls: a
principle of management, which can never
be departed from, with propriety.

The ſuperfluous rain water, or YARD
LIQUOR, of theſe ſeveral yards, paſs off, in
the following manner. That of the dung
yard (as well as thoſe of the inferior yards)
paſſes, firſt, into the principal ſtraw yard;
in a pit, or hollow part, of which it makes
its firſt depoſit. From hence the collected

A a 3   waters

40.
WATERING
YARDS.

FARM YARD
ECONOMY.

YARD
LIQUOR.

40.

YARD
LIQUOR.

waters will be led through paved courts, and a ſtable yard,—collecting in their paſſage, and by proper aſſiſtance, in times of rain, the ſulliage which ſuch places are ever accumulating,—to a common receptacle; where, having depoſited their groſſer feculencies, they will fall immediately into the main float that has been mentioned, mix with its ſtream, and aſſiſt in fertilizing the meadow lands which lie below theſe yards.

INDEX.

INDEX

TO THE

TWO VOLUMES.

A a 4   Arrange-

INDEX.

INDEX.

INDEX.

I N D E X.

B b   Grasslands,

Letting

B b 3   Manage-

INDEX.

B b 4

Occu-

INDEX.

Pilchard

INDEX.

Q.

R.

INDEX.

Remarks

Scalding

Sur-

INDEX.

C c   Tillage,

INDEX.

INDEX.

INDEX.

FINIS.

CPSIA information can be obtained at www.ICGtesting.com
Printed in the USA
LVOW11s1942071213

364269LV00001B/4/P